Praise for *The 15-Minute Method*

"I gut-laughed. I cried. I learned life-changing things. This book will make you wildly productive, and more than that, it will magically transform your experience of being human."
— **Linda Sivertsen**, *New York Times* bestselling coauthor and host of the *Beautiful Writers Podcast*

"I've been coaching creative and performing artists for 35 years. When I ask new clients how much time they'd like to spend each day on the creative project we've been discussing, they almost always say, '20 minutes.' They pick this number for two reasons: 20 minutes seems doable, and they do not want to disappoint themselves by picking a larger number and failing. Sam Bennett knows this territory inside out. Her conviction that spending 15 minutes a day on something important to you can make a huge difference is spot-on. She guarantees it; I do, too. There's nothing like a doable daily practice to help you live your life purposes and get things done. Don't miss this book — and maybe make reading it your daily 15-minute practice!"
— **Eric Maisel**, author of *Coaching the Artist Within* and *The Power of Daily Practice*

"Smart. Generous. Funny as hell. If you want to stop feeling like shit and actually get somewhere good in your life, this book is the guide to get you there. No airy-woo-woo here — just a good, practical, real-life approach that takes into account the heartbreaks and roadblocks we all face from time to time. Don't be deceived by how simple *The 15-Minute Method* sounds, because it actually can change your life for the better."
— **Andrea Owen**, author of *How to Stop Feeling Like Sh\*t* and podcast host

# THE
# 15-MINUTE
# METHOD

# Also by Sam Bennett

*Get It Done: From Procrastination to Creative Genius
in 15 Minutes a Day*

*Start Right Where You Are: How Little Changes Can Make
a Big Difference for Overwhelmed Procrastinators,
Frustrated Overachievers, and Recovering Perfectionists*

# THE
# 15-MINUTE
# METHOD

## THE SURPRISINGLY SIMPLE ART
## OF GETTING IT DONE

## SAM BENNETT

New World Library
Novato, California

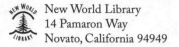

New World Library
14 Pamaron Way
Novato, California 94949

Text design by Tona Pearce Myers

Library of Congress Cataloging-in-Publication Data
Names: Bennett, Sam, date, author.
Title: The 15-minute method : the surprisingly simple art of getting it done / Sam Bennett.
Other titles: Fifteen minute method
Description: Novato, California : New World Library, [2024] | Includes bibliographical references. | Summary: "A friendly, judgment-free guide to taming procrastination, ending overwhelm, finishing projects, and accomplishing goals"-- Provided by publisher.
Identifiers: LCCN 2024010814 (print) | LCCN 2024010815 (ebook) | ISBN 9781608689064 (paperback) | ISBN 9781608689071 (epub)
Subjects: LCSH: Procrastination. | Self-actualization (Psychology) | Decision making.
Classification: LCC BF637.P76 B466 2024 (print) | LCC BF637.P76 (ebook) |DDC 179/.8--dc23/eng/20240422
LC record available at https://lccn.loc.gov/2024010814
LC ebook record available at https://lccn.loc.gov/2024010815

First printing, June 2024
ISBN 978-1-60868-906-4
Ebook ISBN 978-1-60868-907-1
Printed in Canada on 100% postconsumer-waste recycled paper

 New World Library is proud to be a Gold Certified Environmentally Responsible Publisher. Publisher certification awarded by Green Press Initiative.

10   9   8   7   6   5   4   3   2   1

# Contents

## Introduction
# What *Is* the 15-Minute Method?

That's a great question. I can't wait for you to tell me. See, the 15-Minute Method is especially designed to be ultra-personalized, flexible, friendly, and free-flowing.

Here's the basic idea: you spend 15 minutes a day, every single day, doing something that matters to you. After all, you spend pretty much all day doing stuff for other people, is it so outrageous that you take a quarter of an hour for yourself?

Even just the premise is sort of interesting: What *does* matter to you? What matters to you that might also matter to others? Or what matters only to you? When I started giving 15 minutes of my undivided attention each day to things that matter to me, my whole life turned around. I was able to start and grow my own mid-six-figure business, write several books and a hit musical, and maybe most important, gain the skills I needed to face the difficulties that lay ahead. We'll get to that part soon enough. But for now: What matters to *you*?

If you're not sure, keep reading for plenty of opportunities and ideas to figure it out. Clients and students of mine have used their 15 minutes a day to work on a huge array of projects, ranging from clearing off the back porch so it became a beautiful, usable space instead of a dumping ground to completing a baby quilt just in time for that child's high school graduation. For more specifics, see chapter 2, "52 Suggestions of 15-Minute Activities."

All the details are up to you. The 15-Minute Method is meant to work *with* your existing life, in order to help you experience your life more fully. You may think that in order to change your life you need to do something big: move to a new city, get divorced, find a new job, reinvent yourself completely. And then it's all so overwhelming that you don't do anything. What I've found is that little, tiny changes — the kind that you can make in 15 minutes — are enough to move the needle on your levels of joy and satisfaction. And when your joy and satisfaction are up, you might discover that those big changes aren't necessary, or, if they are, that you now have the momentum to make them happen more easily.

If you are the kind of person who likes a strict, logical, step-by-step system, well — this isn't exactly that. It's more of a buffet: take what you like, sample something new, and ignore the stuff you don't care for.

And if you've got an inner-rebel-teenager, "you can't make me" part that sometimes runs the show, congratulations — you have finally found a personal development system that invites you to design your own path, break off from conventional wisdom, and do your own thing.

- Feel free to do your 15 minutes any time you like. No need for a set schedule.
- Feel free to experiment with different activities during your 15 minutes, depending on your mood, energy level, and current circumstances.
- Feel free to take days off, if that feels good.
- Read (or just page through) this book in any order.
- Remember that you can't screw this up. Nor can you get an A+. This is an experiment, and your process and your results are just for you.

If, on the other hand, you're the kind of person who appreciates more of a set plan, let me suggest the following:

- Do your 15 minutes every morning, first thing. Before you check your email. I do mine (a writing prayer/meditation practice) before I even get out of bed.
- Pick one project or activity and stay with it for at least a week, then switch if you like.
- Or make a list of a variety of 15-minute tasks, and pick one each day at random or to suit your mood.
- You might enjoy spending one day per week on an exercise in this book (they're called 15-Minute Experiments, and you'll find one in each chapter), then spending the other six on your own work.
- Again, remember that you can't screw this up. Nor can you get an A+. This is an experiment, and your process and your results are just for you.

Either way, don't be afraid of:

- doing it poorly. Cumulatively, 15 minutes of kinda crappy work can yield great results in the long run.
- not getting anything done. 15 minutes of quiet, of not-doing, or even of boredom, builds character.
- feeling discouraged or disenchanted. Do your 15 minutes anyway, and then see how you feel.
- talking about it with others. Sharing your goals and your process with trusted allies will give you additional energy and accountability.
- *not* talking about it with others. Especially the people in your life who make a hobby out of dream-crushing.
- setting a timer — or not.
- pushing yourself *or* going easy on yourself.
- finding that sometimes your 15 minutes turns into 30 minutes, or several hours. How lovely to get into that flow state.

The idea that you can change your life in just 15 minutes a day would be ridiculous, except it happens to be true. Clearly, if you played guitar for 15 minutes a day, every day for a month or two, you would become a better guitar player. Do that for a few years, and you would become great.

The 100-hour rule, popularized by psychologist Andres Ericsson, says that 100 hours of "deliberate practice" will make you better than 95 percent of the world's population at your chosen discipline. Working for 15 minutes a day, you could potentially become world-class at whatever it is you want to do in only 400 days — or just over a year.

Even if you don't want to be the best at something, it's reassuring to know that you could substantially improve in such a short amount of time.

What I know for sure is that when you do things, things happen.
When you take action, there is a ripple effect.
When you take daily action, there is a compounding ripple effect.
The point is, there is no reason to delay your goals.

When you get to the end of your days, you will be so glad you took the time to make daily progress on the things that really mattered to you and didn't just spend all your days trying to make other people happy (which never works, anyway).

One last thing: this "surprisingly simple" practice of spending 15 minutes on what matters to you can have an outsized effect on your mindset, your relationships, and your income. And while most of these shifts will be welcome, some may lead to deeper inner work, which is not always easy. Remember that you are the agent of change. You can decide to dig in to the more emotionally complex work or to skip the tough stuff, based on whatever's best for you right now. You are free to pick and choose what works for you, and modify or ignore the rest.

Join me at 15MinuteMethod.com/bonus, and let's see how this rolls out, shall we? We can share what we're working on, get support, and cheer each other on. I'll put some additional resources, audios, and worksheets there, too. Fun, right? Cool. See you over there.

You are so good and brave. Thanks for experimenting.

By the way — you look really great today.

# 1
# Opening

To begin, please think of something that you would really like to do.

Without pondering, just think of something — anything — that would make a big difference in your life but that, for whatever reason, you aren't doing.

Maybe you know your life would be better if you got your finances under control, or set yourself up to get a better job. Maybe you'd like to clear out the clutter in your house. Or maybe you'd like to do something like play an instrument, or make art, or write a book.

Whatever your project is, this book suggests that you spend 15 minutes a day, every single day, focusing and working on it (or them, if you decide to shift between projects).

If you feel like you can do that easily on your own — and without giving up after a few sessions — then feel free to put this book down and walk away. Or read it for fun and to pick up a few neat tricks.

If you are like most people I talk with, though, the idea of spending even just 15 minutes a day on something that matters to you brings up a whole raft of objections:

- 15 minutes is not enough time.
- I'm already too busy.

- I don't know where to begin.
- I don't need another project.
- I'm not really qualified.
- I'm concerned that if I accomplish this thing, my life will change.

To which I might ask you: What if the opposite is true?

- What if 15 minutes is the perfect amount of time?
- What if — despite your busy calendar — you find you have plenty of time for something that actually matters to you?
- What if you already know enough to at least begin?
- What if the thing you need most is a project that matters to you?
- What if your curiosity qualifies you?
- What if you accomplish this thing and your life changes in the most delightful ways?

This book came about because my editor asked if I might consider writing a book about overwhelm. Since I've spent the past 20+ years working with people on their productivity, procrastination, and creativity, that's a word I hear a lot, and more and more lately.

I agreed, because overwhelm is one of those deceptive concepts: It seems like an outside problem, but it's actually an inside problem. You are not overwhelmed by your schedule or your tasks; you are overwhelmed by your thinking about those things.

Much like "time management," which is another tricky and overused phrase. Because time management, of course, is not about time.

So most of this book is about the thought patterns, emotional underpinnings, and spiritual uncertainty that create overwhelm, and how to break free of them. And there are also plenty of handy ideas and tips along the way.

But the main gist is this: spend 15 minutes a day, every single day, on something that matters to *you*.

Please note: this 15-minute period is not for catching up on your email, or your paperwork, or any other regular, day-to-day activity. This time is for stretching yourself. It's for having some fun. It's for reconnecting with your own, singular self — the part of you that is not anyone's parent or boss or employee or friend. Ask yourself: What might I do if I had perfect freedom, I didn't need the money, and I knew no one's feelings would get hurt?

I don't care if your 15-minute project matters to anyone else. I don't care if anyone else even knows about it. What I care about is the idea that you fill your own cup first. When you spend 15 minutes a day on something that matters to you, your spirit is revived. You get a glint in your eye and some pep in your step. Your sense of humor returns. You are calmer and more patient. You can feel your own progress as your chain of 15 minutes grows each day, and you gain confidence. You become more joyful.

Contrariwise, here's what can happen when you refuse to find 15 minutes a day for something that matters to you: You feel like you're on a hamster wheel. Permanently exhausted. Drained. Discouraged. Everything feels hard. You push yourself each day to get everything done but still feel like you're falling behind. By the end of the day, you feel so deprived that you stay up late, doomscrolling, staying awake to revenge-grab some time for yourself, even though you know it will only make you more tired tomorrow.

You are creatively starving yourself. And we all know what happens when you let yourself get too hungry. It isn't pretty.

We're going to talk about why there's no such thing as a "good" idea. We'll take a look at some of the hidden patterns that are keeping you held back, and we'll countermand your perfectionism.

There's some cultural programming that's gumming up your inner works as well, and some of these ideas you may find a tad shocking. #cueclutchingofpearls

I've included as many practical tips as I can about getting out from under the piles of stuff, of emails, of everyone else's BS, and some strategies so you can actually start getting what you want.

Because that's what this book is really about: you getting more of what you want, so you can be the happy, thriving, contributing member of our global community that you were born to be.

All in just 15 minutes a day.

## 15-Minute Experiment

Make a short list of things you would like to do but aren't currently doing. Make sure they are things that matter to you (they may or may not matter to anyone else). They can be big, like "Renovate the kitchen," or small, like "Practice hand-lettering." They can be practical, like "Clear out my closet," or fantastical, like "Sing opera in Italy." Have fun and don't censor yourself. You're not committing to anything right now — you're just making a list of things you might like to do. If you already know what you'd like your project to be, you might want to make a list of individual 15-minute steps instead.

## *What If...*

What if you knew with absolute certainty that reading this book (or even just part of it) would turn out to be a turning point in your life? How can you honor yourself today, at the beginning of this transition? Even just giving yourself a quick pat on the back is good.

# 2

# 52 Suggestions of 15-Minute Activities

The following is a list of activities that are free or extremely low-cost, that require little or no equipment or training, and that, if done every day for 15 minutes (or until complete), are guaranteed to change your life.

You could also pick one of these activities to do each day (in no particular order), and that would probably change your life, too.

Which will you pick?

- Take a walk. In 15 minutes, you can probably walk between half a mile and a mile, so in a year, you will have covered between 182 and 365 miles.
- Read a book. Most people can read 9 to 12 pages in 15 minutes, so you could read a 350-page novel in a month.
- Learn to love strength training. Studies show that 15 minutes a day of weight training, high-intensity interval training (HIIT), or even calisthenics (where you use your own body weight to perform an exercise, so you don't need any special equipment) can go a long way to improving health.
- Stretch. My Pilates instructor friend says, "When you stop stretching, you die." Kinda intense, but not untrue — about body, mind, or spirit — right?
- Whittle.

- Prep food. One 15-minute session of chopping gets everything ready for several days' worth of quick lunchtime salads or snacks.
- Call former colleagues to reconnect and network.
- Organize or clear 5 to 10 items from a closet, junk drawer, or any other location where things accumulate.
- Care for houseplants: water, fertilize, transplant, defoliate, mist, dust, caress, whisper sweet nothings.
- Clear old files.
- Clean out a deceased loved one's belongings. Taking it 15 minutes at a time reduces overwhelm and gives plenty of room to have feelings.
- Draw/sketch/paint/color/doodle/Zentangle. The time limit does amazing things to combat self-criticism.
- Needlework. Finally make steady progress on that needlepoint, sewing, or knitting project. Save money by mending old, beloved things. Visible mending is even more fun and artsy.
- Genealogy research.
- Daily self-portrait.
- Play an instrument. Working in short bursts allows you to build hand strength and breath control, and consistent practice will lead to marked improvement.
- Listen to music.
- Train your voice. Practice vocal warm-ups, tongue twisters, or breath control. So useful, even if you are not a speaker or singer.
- Read poetry aloud for the sheer joy of it. Gorgeous.
- Read Shakespeare (also better read aloud).
- Call your BFF for no reason.
- Write to a long-lost friend. Maintaining relationships can get harder as we get older, but having a circle of old

friends who share our memories is a blessing beyond price.

- Check in with a young person.
- Check in with an older person.
- Pet, play with, or otherwise communicate with the animals in your life. Clean their bowls, groom them, play enriching games, give them your focus and love.
- Skin-care regime. Whether you go all in with a system of lotions and potions or just enjoy 15 minutes of facial massage (gua sha, anyone?), you can improve your circulation and your overall vibrancy.*
- Self-massage / acupressure / Reiki / foot massage / fascia release.
- Dance.
- Prep for the next day: lay out your clothes; gather any notes, books, phone numbers, or other needed materials; check maps/routes — anything to prevent last-minute rushing around.
- Spend an extra 15 minutes on your appearance. Most people wear 20 percent of their wardrobe 80 percent of the time. Which means you've probably got some lovely articles of clothing that could be combined to make a groovy new look. Or maybe you'd like to change up your hair or makeup routine, if you have one.
- Meditation practice. Prayer, chanting, walking or seated

---

* I'm a bit agog at how much some skin-care stuff costs, and I have no idea if any of it works, as I've always shopped in the cheap-and-cheerful department when it comes to beauty. Here's what I think is interesting: I know way more about various serums, lotions, and cleansers that I'll never buy than I know about, say, investment strategies. That's partly due to the media's insistence that my looks matter more than my financial acumen, and partly because I simply haven't made the effort to learn about investing. Perhaps that will be my new 15-minute project? Hmm.

meditation, breathing, listening to guided meditations on an app...there is no wrong way to commune with the divine. As Rumi reminds us, "Let the beauty we love be what we do. There are hundreds of ways to kneel and kiss the ground."

- Study astronomy, geology, marine biology, anatomy — anything that increases your understanding of how the natural world works.
- Pay attention to your money. Maybe start with setting up automatic withdrawals to savings, investments, an IRA, charitable donations, etc. Review expense reports, P&Ls, subscriptions, credit card bills, and auto-debits to make sure you're not paying for things you're not using. Review long-term financial plans.
- Daily orgasm.
- Get outside and quietly enjoy the sky, the wind, the clouds.
- Garden.
- Discover more about business, marketing, investing — it's a great way to learn about human behavior.
- Make something with your hands. Studies show that hands-on creativity can lift your mood, help alleviate depression, and help your brain better cope with emotions. Skill level doesn't matter — it's the doing of it that helps.
- Update LinkedIn or another professional profile.
- Take photographs or organize the ones you've already got.
- Focus on the tricky bits of anything you want to get better at: If it's golf, practice just your putting, or if you love soccer, work on hitting a first-time volley. Practice the verb tenses of the language you're learning. Rehearse the complicated parts of your speech or script

or song until they become second nature. Mastering the finer details will lead to greater proficiency.

- Update your CV or résumé.
- Ask for — or give — a testimonial or referral.
- Social media posts. Take five minutes to scan your feed, five minutes to pose a thoughtful question or share a recent piece of work, and another five to comment on other people's posts.
- Study an unfamiliar religion or philosophy.
- Learn a language.
- Watch TED Talks.
- Study self-defense: mental, verbal, physical, spiritual…
- Write a love letter.
- Write a thank-you note.
- Make a list of lovely, precious, or unexpected moments you experienced that day. The smile from the nice bus driver, the first bite of buttered toast, the surprise compliment you gave or received.
- Write a book. If you don't second-guess yourself too much, you can probably write about 250 words in 15 minutes, so in six months, that's 45,000 words, which is a book.

## 15-Minute Experiment

You pick one of the above. And do it.

## What If…

What if you remember that the sparkle in your eye when you've done your 15 minutes makes you irresistibly appealing all day long?

# 3

# Your Zone of Creative Genius

I often use the word *creative*, and I know that might turn some people off. Somehow the world has conflated the words *creative* and *artistic*. But those two things are not synonyms.

*Creative* refers to the talent of innovative problem-solving. *Artistic* refers to a talent in the arts.

Not everyone is artistic. Everyone is creative.

We are all creating, all the time. We create dairy-free meals and vacation plans and holiday parties. We create stories about people we see on the street. We create homes and knitting patterns and lifelong friendships and family traditions and in-jokes. Our creations make up our world.

You may think that because you don't make visual art, write, or perform, you are not creative. Or maybe you think creative people are kind of weird. (To which I say: Honey, everyone is weird. Embrace your weird.)

Everyone is creative, and more than that, everyone has a Zone of Creative Genius.*

If you are wondering what your Zone of Creative Genius is, answer these questions swiftly and without pondering:

---

\* Hat tip to Gay Hendricks and his groundbreaking work on Zones of Genius in both *The Big Leap* and *The Genius Zone*. Both are great reads.

1. What's the one thing I love doing, no matter what?
2. What's something I've always been naturally good at?
3. What's something that other people praise me for, but I think isn't that big of a deal?
4. What's something that, if someone woke me up at 3 a.m. and said, "Hey, we're going to go do XYZ right now," I would be up in a flash and looking for my shoes?
5. What's something that I spend quite a bit of money and time on, and my family and friends think it's a bit crazy?

If you're still not sure, consider this: In every office I've ever been in, there is a "birthday person." The birthday person is someone in the office who takes it upon themselves to keep track of everyone's birthday and make sure there's a card and cupcakes in the break room. And if you ask them if they mind the extra work, they'll say, "Oh, no! I like doing this. It's fun for me."

That birthday person has a natural gift for celebration and an ability to make people feel special. That's their Zone of Creative Genius. And if that person wanted to start a business, they might do well to leverage this gift for getting the party started and go into the events business. Or perhaps they'd do well in HR, creating policies and practices that help employees feel seen, heard, and valued.

You can also think of your Zone of Creative Genius this way: If you have ever solved a problem differently than anyone else has ever solved the problem, congratulations — you are a creative genius. And the way in which you solved the problem is the key to your Zone of Creative Genius.

Most people have a few Zones of Creative Genius. Highly creative people have multiple Zones of Creative Genius. They are naturally good at a lot of things. You may know someone like that — the artistic ones are pretty easy to spot, but the non-artistic highly creative people are often hiding in plain sight.

You might be especially good at communicating with animals. You might have a gift for giving compliments that make others feel seen. Your creativity might express itself in a gift for systems, or numbers, or logic, or skepticism.

Your Zones of Creative Genius might go unnoticed by you, because they come so naturally. You might want to make a running list of hobbies you've loved, documentaries that fascinate you, odd fixations, and compliments you get that cause you to think to yourself, "But everyone is like this, aren't they?" (nope — they aren't) and see if you can find some commonalities.

Also, you might want to ask some trusted friends the things they've noticed you are good at.

Figuring out your one or more Zones of Creative Genius can be a helpful step in determining how you want to spend your 15 minutes a day.

## 15-Minute Experiment

Make a list of all the hobbies, talents, and interests you have, or have had, in your life. Can you find a throughline? Might you want to revisit any of those activities?

## What If...

What if you have been seriously underestimating yourself — and your genius — this whole time?

# 4

# Joe Polish and Me

I once heard a keynote delivered by Joe Polish, master marketer and addiction-recovery advocate, and he listed a bunch of activities that, if you did any of them every day for a month, would be 100 percent guaranteed to change your life for the better.

I remember one was getting up and doing 25 burpees each morning. If you don't know, burpees are a military-style full-body exercise that consists of starting on your hands and knees, then thrusting your legs back into a push-up, then jumping forward into a squat, and then springing up all the way with your hands in the air. If you can't jump or do a squat-thrust, you can sort of walk your way through it, as I do, and look like a drunken panda. Nevertheless, it is very effective for full-body conditioning and strength building, and doing 25 a day would certainly improve your physical and mental well-being, as it is hella hard, and doing hard things almost inevitably improves oneself.

He also suggested that a person could get a massage every day. I nearly gasped. Is that even legal? But when I think of the good ideas I have on the massage table, it makes sense to invest in that. And imagine how much great work a skilled body-worker could do if I were there every day, instead of just going once every ten months, when I'm already so stressed-out you could bounce a quarter off my traps. Even twice a week for a month could be a game changer. I'm still considering this one.

The other suggestion I remember is the beauty and magic of sending a thank-you note each day. Now, this is something I can really get behind. I come from a whole family of monogrammed-stationery-having thank-you note writers. I tell people all the time that if you reach out to just one person a day, especially in the form of a thank-you, you will completely transform your business and your life.

Then Joe Polish added that if any of us here in the audience sent him a thank-you note, he would send us a gift in return. He said, "I can give out my private email, because almost none of you will ever do this."

And apparently he was right. Even I, little miss queen of the monogrammed thank-you notes, never once wrote him back. Nor did I start doing more burpees or getting more massages.

Why? What keeps us from taking the steps that could really make a difference?

What if I had written Joe Polish and then we became pen pals and besties, and now he was willing to endorse this book?

Obvs, didn't happen, but still: a worthwhile inquiry.

## 15-Minute Experiment

Reflect on these questions:

- What's an open invitation that you ignored or turned down?
- Why?
- How might you handle this situation next time?

## What If...

What if success lies in both making yourself more uncomfortable than you care to (burpees) and much more comfortable than you are used to (massages)?

# 5

# Be Ready

Years ago, I was sitting at my desk, unshowered and in my grubby sweats, when I saw a brief notification online that Donna Karan would be having a book signing of her autobiography, *My Journey*, at a bookstore in Montecito, just a few miles from where I was living.

Now, Donna Karan is one of my all-time creative heroes. I love everything about her story — from her bravery in stepping in as lead designer to take over the Anne Klein line when her mentor Ms. Klein died, to her Seven Easy Pieces line of "essentials."* To my mind, Donna Karan understands what I truly want and need my clothes to be.

In addition, Donna Karan's label is one of the few that are designed for taller women, so ever since high school, whenever I had a special occasion and needed something fancy, I always ended up in the Donna Karan section of the department store. Her clothes got me through some of the most important, memorable (and, as a shy, introverted person who does not enjoy dressing up at all — stressful) events of my life.

OK, so here we are — one of my heroes is going to be practically around the corner in just a few hours, and I am nowhere

---

\* I even love her current Urban Zen line, even though it stops at a size 14, which, as a size 18, I find super annoying. But I forgive her, because I love her.

near ready. But I wrote a book called *Get It Done*, and I spend all day, every day, telling people to do what scares them. Plus, I've got a lifetime of last-minute auditions as practice.* I hopped in the shower, threw on a nice outfit, and jumped in the car.

When I got to the bookstore, there were a bunch of flamingos milling around.

OK, not actual flamingos.

But rather a flock of expensively dressed former models. Of course. Who do fashion designers know? Models. What happens to models when they stop modeling? They take their hard-earned money (make no mistake — modeling is damn hard work) and marry someone successful and move to Montecito.

The flamingos and I stood obediently in line. And the outfit I had been so proud of having clean and ready just half an hour ago seemed sort of sad next to the skinny jeans worn with shoes that I knew cost more than my rent and luscious, luxurious "oh this old thing?" six-ply cashmere sweaters being slung around. Around me was lots of chatter about this or that charity event and how nice it was in Gstaad over the holidays. The "One of These Things Is Not Like the Others" song started to play in my head. I felt so awkward. But I stayed.

As the line moved forward, I took a big, groovy orange cardboard envelope out of my bag. It was shaped like a FedEx

---

* This seems as good a time as any to mention that I spent most of my life working as an actor. I did my first play in kindergarten. I went to theater camp. I did all the shows in school, and eventually ended up working at Chicago's legendary improv/sketch comedy theatre, the Second City. I had a pretty darn good career in LA, appearing on shows like *The Drew Carey Show*, *Days of Our Lives*, and *Modern Family*. So, yeah — I have a lot of experience pulling myself together at the last minute to drive across town and pretend to be someone else.

envelope, and it had my tagline, "By the Way, You Look Really Great Today," printed on the outside. Inside the envelope I had put two copies of my book, the aforementioned *Get It Done*, whose cover is also orange, so it all looked kind of branded and pulled together.

When I got through the line up to where Ms. Karan was sitting, I crouched down in front of the table to be at eye level with her. As she started to sign my book, I said, "Hi — I was so happy to get a copy of your book, and so I brought you a copy of mine." She looked at me — eyebrows up. "You brought me *your* book? You wrote a book?"

"Yes," I said, handing her the envelope. "And actually, there's two copies — one to keep and one to give away."

"Oh," she said, a bit blankly. "That's very nice of you." She handed the envelope of books off to her assistant. "Cool envelope."

"Thanks. I just wanted to say thank you," I said. And my voice started to quaver and tears started to roll down my face. "Your work has meant so much to me...and...just...thank you."

"You're welcome," she said.

I walked away so I wouldn't hold up the line, and also so I could go blubber somewhere less conspicuous.

I drove home, still blubbering, and in the driveway, I finally looked at the inscription:

> *To Sam — So sweet.*
> *Hope you enjoy 'My Journey.'*
> *Good luck on your book.*
> *Eternally, from Donna.*

More blubs.

To be clear, that is the end of the story. Donna and I did not become pen pals or besties. But I did end up with an excellent teaching story for my clients. When I told them the story, I said, "So how many of you could be ready in half an hour to meet your hero? Do you have an outfit, an up-to-date haircut, and, if appropriate, a flattering makeup routine? If needed, are your marketing materials up to snuff?"

I'm not saying everything has to be all perfecty-schmerfecty all the time, but, as they say, dress for the job you want. Prepare for the future you want. Because certainly, failing to do so will give you a future you do not want, yes?

## 15-Minute Experiment

Extrapolate this story for your own circumstances:

- If your dream job came up suddenly, could you be ready to be first in line to interview?
- If you had a chance to sell your house at a big profit, could you be ready to move quickly?
- If you are looking for love, are your home and heart open and available?

## *What If...*

What if you approached your 15 minutes today with the same heart-pounding enthusiasm you would feel if you were meeting a personal hero, or a clandestine lover?

# 6

# Is It a Good Idea?

You should know that there is no such thing as a "good" idea. So...you should stop waiting to have one.

All ideas are just ideas.

And you have them all the time. You can't help it. You are a nonstop fountain of ideas.

So this "I can't think of anything" is untrue. You have thought of things, but you've rejected them. You've had ideas; you just didn't like them or didn't think that others would like them.

Please remember that the idea you start with is not final — it's just a place to start. The first stop on the bus is not the destination.

But if you feel like your idea could use some scrutiny, ask yourself some or all of these questions and see what insights emerge:

### Is This a "Good" Idea?
1. Have I ever done anything like this before?
2. If so, how did that go? What did I learn?
3. To act on this idea, what might some initial 15-minute tasks be?
4. How do I feel about taking those steps?

5. How speculative is this project? On a scale of 1 to 5, how likely am I to be able to pull it off?

6. How much will the success of this project depend on other people's support, acceptance, approval, or cooperation? How much of the success is entirely within my own control?

7. Do I think that pursuing this idea will be worth it just for the experience?

8. Am I eager to be the person I'll need to become in order to pull this off?

9. What are my good/better/best visions of success for this project?

10. Any other considerations or prevailing conditions to factor in? For example, if you want to start a business but you've just had a baby, you might need to make some special arrangements, hire additional help, or devise a delightfully unusual business plan that accommodates your new family member.

## 15-Minute Experiment

As you consider moving forward on your idea, spend 15 minutes noodling or doodling on this thought: What will I say to myself when I feel tired or overwhelmed or want to quit?

## What If...

What if success turns out to be embarrassingly easy?

# 7

# Skip the First Step, and Other Unusual Strategies

Here are some unconventional approaches to getting started on a project or goal. They are especially useful when you've been putting something off for a long time, when you have to start over, or when there's a big emotional component to the work.

## Keep a Productivity/Rest Diary

Getting a baseline understanding of how much rest you need (and at what time of day) to achieve maximum sustainable productivity can be illuminating. Much like logging what you eat and drink in a food diary, keeping a productivity/rest diary is designed to focus your attention on how much rest you are actually getting, whether you find it actually restful, and how much you need to function at your best.

You can set this up in any way that makes sense to you: use a tracking app of some kind or just pen and paper. See if you can make some notes throughout the day about how much rest/restorative time you give yourself, as well as when and how you are most productive. You may find that you love to write or create in the mornings and save the afternoons for more administrative tasks. You may find that an afternoon siesta causes you to work more efficiently the rest of the day, or that a daily 15-minute walk eliminates your 3 p.m. slump.

You may also discover that the activities you think of as "taking a break," like playing a game on your phone, cruising social media, or reading the news, are actually depleting you.

In time, you will begin to trust yourself around your rest/work balance and even find that doing your meaningful work for 15 minutes a day counts as both work and rest.

## Skip the First Step

Oftentimes when facing a big new project, we can get ourselves stuck by deciding that the first step has to be something monumental — too big, too extreme, or too tedious.

For example, if you want to write a novel, you decide the first step is to go back to school and get an MFA (too big). If you want to spend more time in nature, you decide the first step is to sell the house and move to a cabin in the woods (too extreme). Or if you want to make a photo scrapbook for Mom's 80th birthday, you decide the first step is to organize the boxes and boxes of photos by putting them in chronological order (too tedious).

To counteract this, whatever you think the second step might be — consider starting there instead. So maybe it's "write a summary of the plot" or "go hiking in the woods" or "start picking out ten of your favorite photos."

This is also a good tactic for those whose inner teenagers immediately resist all goals, suggestions, or plans. Just sneak in the side door and start with a janky, half-baked plan. Could be fun.

## Capture Ideas as They Come

Start making notes about your idea or project on index cards or using a note-taking app. I find whole pieces of paper to be intimidating (what if I don't use up the whole sheet? Isn't that wasteful?), and I can never find anything I've written in a journal. But the ability to capture little bits of ideas, quotes, points of inquiry, and vague notions and keep them all together in no particular order is...how this book got written. It's also how I run my business, bought a house, wrote a musical, and stay in touch with a large network of amazing people.

## Pretend You Are Already an Expert

Want to start painting? Just start! Assume you already know more than you think you do. Pretend you are a born genius and begin painting with great confidence and joy. You'll learn as you go. Same with poetry, writing, playing music, creating a TV show, designing a game board, sewing, and anything else you feel is locked behind some impenetrable gate of specialized knowledge.

Honestly, a lot of my successes came about because I didn't know that what I was trying was supposed to be hard. So I just took a swing, ignored conventional wisdom, broke some of the stupider rules, and obeyed my own instincts and good taste. There have been a few crash-and-burns, but mostly it's worked out great, and it makes my life way more interesting than if I'd waited to become an expert.

Obviously, it's easier to try this when the consequences of failure are mild. I wouldn't swing into real estate investing without doing some research, nor would I start preparing raw pufferfish just for giggles. But for many of the things you want to try, you could probably just dive in and see what happens.

All this "getting ready to get ready" stuff is just cluttering up your path, right?

## Give Yourself Frequent Rewards

Write a sentence = get a chocolate chip.
Clear out the sock drawer = watch some kitten videos.
Make a difficult phone call = enjoy a cup of that fancy coffee or tea or whatever.

You wouldn't expect a child to do something hard without some praise or reward, would you? Or ask an employee to take on a challenging project without some recompense? So start giving yourself special prizes — big and small.

I also make a point of buying myself something special whenever I hit a big milestone. Sometimes it's something I was probably going to buy anyway, but naming it in my mind as my "Signed My Publishing Contract Gold Charm Necklace" or my "Opening Night of My Musical Designer Tote" is extra fun.*

## Start at the End

What's the end result you are hoping for from your project? Can you just start there?

If not, can you reverse engineer from there?

## Quit Rushing In (aka Rest First)

Rather than think, "I've got so much to do — I'll get it all done and then rest," which of course never works because you're never actually done, why not try resting first? Take 15 minutes to have a bite to eat, read something enjoyable, take a short nap or a brief walk — anything that refreshes you.

---

\* I thrifted the tote, which only increases its specialness to me.

And to those of you who are thinking, "Nope — if I sit down to read or nap or rest, I'll never get up again," I want to remind you that these are the words of a person who is starved for rest. Once you start giving your body and mind the frequent breaks you actually need, you won't feel so timorous. Nor will you fall into the trap of binge-watching reruns or other late-night tactics that have you staying awake when you're exhausted simply because you feel so deprived of anything fun or me-time focused.

Here's an idea that fascinates me: What if before beginning anything hard or complicated, you approached it as you might a stray dog that you were trying to befriend? What if, instead of plunging right into clearing out the garage, you sat down and just sort of took it in? Maybe had a mug of something warming and sat quietly? See if the project can speak to you and tell you what it needs.

This "resting first" is different from displacement activities, which are what happens when you know you need to do something, but it stresses you out so much that you redirect your attention to something meaningless, like a video game or other time waster. This is not about mindless deferment; it's about making a conscious decision to be rested and energized before you begin. To ease into your activity, as though you were shopping at an old, slow country market, where it would be considered rude to shop without stopping to gossip, browsing around, and having a cup of coffee while you're there.

I've been living with long-haul Covid for the past 18 months, so this question has taken on a whole new meaning for me. Everything I do depletes my energy (sometimes taking a shower is as much as I can do in a day) and nothing I do restores it. Taking a walk or exercising in any way used to help recharge my batteries, but now it spirals me down into a two- or three-day nap, from which I do not wake up refreshed — if you're curious, it's called post-exertional malaise, and it fucking sucks.

So now this is the way I live:

1. I think of something that needs doing.
2. I check myself. Am I tired? Thirsty? Have I eaten recently? How's my breathing?
3. I contemplate the task for a bit. Does it really need doing? Does it need to be done today? Does it need to be done by me, or can I farm it out to someone?
4. I check the time and set a possible end point — say, "It's 2:30 p.m., so I'll work until 4."
5. Then I quit at quitting time, whether I'm tired or not.

It's a far cry from the *Do! Do! Do!* accomplishment junkie I once was.

And if there has been a spiritual lesson to this disease, perhaps it's to separate my self-worth from my doing. My productivity does not get to determine my self-image anymore. I have discovered that I can run an entire business in 15-minute increments. Heck, I wrote this whole book that way.

When I was working full-time as an actor, I would always give myself a private moment before my entrance onstage. I would touch the wall, take a breath, and recite a short poem to myself. That intentional pause of less than a minute served me well, causing me to center myself, focus, and send myself a signal that it was time to be fully present.

Your rest needn't be long, but it does need to be intentional.

## 15-Minute Experiment

Consider which of the above suggestions you might be willing to try and which ones strike you as just plain silly. Then try one, or, if the timing is off, try writing a brief plan of action for how you might incorporate it into your life or project. I might recommend trying the silliest ones first. Do it, then write me back (Sam@TheRealSamBennett.com) and let me know how it goes, OK?

## *What If...*

What if you secretly bought yourself a little present today? (Shhhh, don't tell anyone...)

# 8

# What Your Excuses Really Mean

You've been making the same excuses for a while now, and I think it's time I shared with you some alternative translations for those excuses.

They are not in any particular order, and some of them repeat or overlap. Read them through — maybe read them aloud — and see which ones resonate for you.

After each excuse, you'll find a suggestion for a 15-Minute Experiment you can try in order to play around with your thinking and get yourself unstuck. Or feel free to invent your own.

A few of these include a practice I call the "90-second doodle." This isn't art — it's just a way to get your thoughts out of your head and onto a piece of paper where you can gain a new perspective on them. So use stick figures, shapes, colors, whatever — just doodle for 90 seconds without stopping or judging yourself.

### *"Now's not a good time." = I'd rather quit than fail.*

Make a list of five things you've done in your life before you felt ready that worked out. Add five things you've never done but wish you had. Now list five things you've decided not to do, and you're glad about it. Review this list for insights, inspiration, and new ideas.

*"I'm not really qualified." = It feels safer to discredit myself than to try.*

Make a list of three people who are, technically, unqualified to do what they do. What do they have to teach you today?

*"I don't know how to do that." = I'm unwilling to trust my inner knowing.*

Write down five innate talents and gifts you've always had. What happens when you trust them?

*"I don't know how to do that." = I'm unwilling to ask an expert.*

Do five to ten minutes of research and find at least three trustworthy people you could ask. Then ask one.

*"What if people see me fail?" = Public opinion is more important than my self-growth.*

Make a graph or doodle delineating exactly how much public scorn you think you could take before you quit. Is it one critical social media comment? Ten? Having two or more acquaintances gossiping about you? People picketing outside your house? Have fun imagining the worst, and see if your fear doesn't lighten up a bit.

*"What if I fail and screw everything up?" = I cannot greet my mistakes with grace.*

90-second doodles: First, please doodle the *feeling* of being criticized for making a mistake. Draw for 90 seconds only. Take a look and notice what you see in that doodle. Next, draw what it might feel like to greet your mistakes with grace. Keep drawing this feeling for 90 seconds. Notice and write down any insights.

*"What if I make big mistakes? Or even little ones?"* = *If I am not perfect, I will not be loved.*

Make a list of 10 people you adore, admire, and respect. Consider whether or not they are perfect. Consider whether or not they believe you are perfect. Reconsider the role of perfection as it relates to love.

*"What if this doesn't turn out right?"* = *I need to know the exact outcome before I begin.*

Answer this in your journal: How's that insistence on trying to predict every result working for you? Has there been a time when something turned out completely differently than you imagined and still entirely perfect?

*"It feels weird to be a beginner."* = *I feel foolish.*

I recommend that you make a habit of feeling foolish. When I'm working with leaders, I encourage them to do something each week at which they are a beginner. Some activity in which they are not in charge, don't already know everything, and often feel like a failure. Whether it's piano lessons or weightlifting or birdwatching, there is a wonderful benefit to spending time in "beginner's mind." Consider your foolish moments a blessing. Spend at least 15 minutes doing something that makes you feel foolish today. (Karaoke, anyone?)

*"What if I don't get it done and it's all a big waste of time?"* = *I value output over process.*

Write this out: What's the minimum result you would need to see in order to feel like this project is worth it? What if the project only ends up yielding half of that? What if it ends up being ten times that? Is it really the output that matters? If so, how can you set yourself up for a guaranteed result?

*"I don't want to waste my time." = I am not curious about who I might become as I do this.*

Imagine your project before you. What does it look like? A box? A treasure chest? A fire? A brick wall? Now, ask your project, "Who do you need me to become?" or, "Who are you inviting me to become?" Be quiet, let the answer bubble up, and write it down.

*"What if it's a waste of time?" = I believe it is possible to "waste" time.*

Time is the infinite now. Time stretches and folds. We experience a lifetime in a moment's glance, and a first kiss is forever. Write down at least three ways in which you experience time. Examine the question, "Is it possible to waste time?"

*"I'm not sure where to start." = I'm afraid to start because I'm afraid I won't see it through.*

Oh, the land of half-finished projects! There's no shame in giving up on something if it doesn't interest you anymore. You are even allowed to get rid of the evidence, instead of feeling bad. Clean out that closet with the old painting supplies and the incomplete scrapbooks. I want to say, "Babe, lighten up. You just need to start somewhere — anywhere — and see how it feels. I give you full permission to quit tomorrow."

*"I've done a lot of research, but I don't know where to start." = I do know where to start, but I can tell that starting will change things in my life, and it feels safer to claim ignorance and stay stuck.*

People often say that "change is hard." In my experience, change isn't nearly as hard as the anticipation of change. You are already changing, so you might as well lean into the process, right? Make a list of three positive outcomes that might occur if you quit fighting the change that is emergent.

*"I don't know anyone who's done anything like this." = I think people will disapprove of me if I do this.*

One of our strongest human desires is to belong, and it is entirely natural to be concerned about the approval and disapproval of others. So let's get specific. Make a list of the particular people who might scoff at you, and exactly what their disapproval means to you. I suppose what I'm getting at is, do you really care about the lack of support from people who probably aren't that supportive no matter what you do?

*"I don't want to start and then not finish." = If I do so much as five minutes of internet research on this, I will have committed myself to this project forever and ever.*

Remind yourself that this is an *experiment* and that spending 15 minutes is not making a lifetime vow. Try to get into a spirit of play, investigation, and wonder. Make a 90-second doodle about how it feels to be weighed down by commitment.

*"I don't have the time for that now." = I refuse to prioritize that.*
Work on it for 15 minutes *today*.

*"With the family, the job, and everything, I don't have a minute to myself." = It's important that I put everyone else's needs ahead of mine.*

I notice that my clients and students who make time for their 15-minute activities show up to their other obligations happier and do them better. Why not try it for a week or ten days and see how you feel? Start today.

*"I want to do it, but I'm so busy with everything else." = It is more important for me to keep my promises to other people than it is to keep my promises to myself.*

Let's use this sense of social responsibility, shall we? I recommend getting a "buddy" or some kind of group accountability. Currently in my business, we offer a subscription to a Daily Practicum.* So every weekday, we all meet online, say hi, and then put our heads down and concentrate for 15 minutes. When the timer goes off, people are positively glowing. You can also partner with a loving, respectful, supportive friend who won't let you get away with your regular shenanigans. You could even start your own group. Heck, you could even start your own group and charge for it. For example, "I wanted to make sure I took a walk every day, so I started the Daily Walkaroos Club. We meet each morning at 6:30 a.m. and walk for 15 minutes. Everyone pays $10/month, and since we now have 15 members, we vote each month on where to donate our $150." Spend 15 minutes today brainstorming on what mode of accountability might work best for you, then take the first step to institute it.

*"I'm always so busy. I just don't have room for anything new." = I prefer the devil I know, thank you very much.*

Let's examine that pernicious schedule of yours: Identify at least one thing that you do regularly that just isn't working for

---

\*     Please check out 15MinuteMethod.com/bonus for free access to this and other helpful tools.

you. Can you cancel it? Can you find anything in your life that you could cancel or amend permanently? I mean, we're only talking about finding 15 minutes a day, right?

*"I'd love to, but I just don't have the time for that." = I refuse to make time for that.*

Claim your power. If you don't want to make time for something, say that. Rather than saying, "I'm too busy," try saying, "I'm choosing not to spend time on that right now." You are not a victim of time. Make a 90-second doodle about what it feels like to take 100 percent responsibility for how you spend your time.

*"I'm going to do that later / after the summer / once the kids graduate / when I retire." = I believe that I will live long enough, and always be healthy enough, to explore my inspirations.*

One of the reasons I started my business is because I am acutely aware that we are not here for very long, and I cannot stand the idea of someone leaving this earth with their song unsung. We do not have an unlimited amount of time to bring our dreams to life, and, moreover, we do not know how long our bodies will be strong enough to do our work. Every time I hear about some freak accident, like a plane landing smack on someone's house or someone being killed by a falling icicle, I say a prayer that they were able to spend time on the things they loved and did not leave behind a long list of "someday I will…" dreams. Spend 15 minutes today figuring out how you can move forward on one of your "someday" dreams.

*"I'm going to do that later / after the summer / once the kids graduate / when I retire." = I save the "good" china for special occasions and rarely wear my best things. The time for "special" is always sometime in the future.*

Find a way to make each day special. You could wear your good shoes.* You could treat yourself to a nicer lunch. You could call someone you miss or practice your origami. Anything that makes today a bit more fancy, more enjoyable, and more delightful counts. Never delay joy.

*"I can't afford that." = I refuse to invest in that.*

Poor money — always getting blamed for our lack of fun. Aside from people who have chronic rent-and-grocery issues, I notice that most people — no matter how broke they feel — find the money for the things that matter to them. So if you're not willing to pay for XYZ, that's fine — but be honest about it, at least to yourself. Rather than say, "I can't afford that," say, "I'm choosing not to put funds toward that right now." Perhaps scan through your latest bank or credit card statement and double-check that you are spending your money in ways that actually matter to you. If, upon further reflection, you decide your project is worth investing in, identify some purchases that you could perhaps scale back on to make more funds available.

---

* When my business reached its tenth anniversary some years ago, as the CEO, I decided it was important to recognize the CEO's contributions to the success of the business. So I bought myself a pair of delightfully expensive, buttery soft, classic Gucci loafers. Every time I put them on, I feel swanky. Consequently, I wear them all the time. I've already had them resoled once, and I'm about to need to do that again. What a fantastic investment I made with those shoes — a true gift from my business to me.

*"I want to do it, but I can't seem to get started." = I am used to disappointing myself.*

Make a list of three to five times when you have kept a promise to yourself. Make some notes about what worked and how you were able to persevere. Now, pick something today that is simple and important only to you, and promise yourself you'll do it. Watch yourself as you either do it or wiggle out of it. Don't get angry with yourself — be compassionate and just notice your process. Try again tomorrow. And the next day. And the next.

*"What if it's great and then that puts too much pressure on me?" = Success is scary and threatening.*

Congratulations on your vivid imagination. But if you are going to imagine an outcome, why not imagine a fabulous outcome? Make a few 90-second doodles about what "scary" success looks like, and then make a few about what "happy" success might look like.

*"What if people think I'm too big for my britches?" = Conformity is better than authenticity.*

Almost every culture has some version of "Don't think you're so special." "The tall poppy gets cut down." "The nail that stands up will get hammered down." And in Scandinavia, the Law of Jante is a whole ethos based on "Don't think you are smarter / better / more important…" I think we can all agree that modesty is, overall, a good thing and that remaining humble to our work is essential. But taking time for things that matter to us is not arrogant; it's authentic. And developing our skills and talents is not boastful; it's honoring our gifts. Because the more we evolve into our true selves, the more we have to share with the rest of the world. Spend 15 minutes humbly developing your authentic self today.

*"How do I know if this is a good idea or not?"* = *I believe there is such a thing as a "good" idea.*

There is no such thing as a good idea. There are just ideas you pursue and ideas you don't. Ideas only prove their merit in execution. Write down three questions you could ask to test-drive your idea — for example, "Has anyone else succeeded at this idea?" "What do the experts say about this kind of thing?" and, "Why does this idea frighten me?"

*"I'm just not sure if this is a good idea or not."* = *I am miserable, and if I start spending time on something that truly matters to me, I'm afraid it's going to show me all the things in my life that make me unhappy, and that will upset the whole applecart, so I think it's better to stay in indecision.*

I'm going to let you come up with your own experiment for this one.

## What If...

What if you never needed anyone's approval ever again? What if all the approval you've already gotten is all you've ever needed?

# 9

# Your Inner Underachiever
# Would Like a Word with You

You have been raised to believe that it is important that you do well.

Moreover, you have been raised to believe that it is important that you *be seen* to do well.

A friend once challenged me to put money in a barista's tip jar when the barista wasn't looking. So far, I have managed to do this exactly twice. I was appalled, but not surprised, by how much I wanted to be witnessed in my tipping. Here is our new Zen koan: If a five-dollar bill falls into a tip jar, but a minimum-wage worker is not there to see it, do I still get credit for being a good person?

I know that some of my readers identify as busy bees, achievement junkies, people pleasers, girl scouts, boy scouts, non-binary scouts, and any other type that might be inclined to put other people's needs ahead of their own well-being. There's nothing wrong with being a good, law-abiding, tax-paying, polite do-gooder in the world. Far from it. But what if this bias toward do-gooder-ism is actually holding you back?

What if your desire to be a "good person" means that you:

- don't allow yourself to try new things?
- don't take risks?

- give up too soon on new ideas?
- are often overdoing, even when your work goes unappreciated?
- are so caught up in the myth of safety that you insulate yourself from life itself?

I want to pass on a beautiful piece of advice that my dear friend, former husband, and beloved poet of the obscene Stephen once gave me. He was noticing how many people were calling me to fix their problems (for free) and how I was often tired and depleted from all this unpaid labor.

"Sam," he said, "have you noticed that almost no one ever bothers *me* with their problems?* Here's my simple three-part system to guarantee that no one ever takes advantage of you again." And then he said that the next time somebody asked me to work for free, I should:

---

* The especially funny part is that what he was saying isn't true — while he sometimes gives strangers the idea that he is indifferent to their approval, Stephen is absolutely the person his friends call when they need help with anything, from building a new roof deck to writing the perfect groomsman's speech. He is intensely loyal, and ferocious in his dedication to the people, animals, places, and activities that he loves. But his thin veneer of not caring serves to protect him from being taken casually for granted by others. Make sense?

One time I asked him to contribute to a homemade advice book I was compiling for a friend's baby shower. (It's a great project, by the way: You just ask people to write or send in a sentence or a paragraph of advice for the expecting parents, newlyweds, college grads, etc., and assemble it into a book. There are always some terrific words of wisdom, and it makes a lovely memento as the years go on.) Stephen's advice to this not-yet-born boy child was this:

*People love you. Let them.*

1. fuck shit up.
2. whine and cry.
3. show up stoned.

I laughed out loud, as I was meant to. Aside from it being a great joke, I wondered if his clever system might contain some important lessons. It was a tantalizing idea: What if the apple polisher in the front row suddenly started sprawling out in the back, passing notes, and making rude jokes? What if I had the kind of persona where people wouldn't even ask for my help? Could I sacrifice my identity as "permanently helpful" with some strategic incompetence?

"Fuck shit up. Whine and cry. Show up stoned" became one of my favorite running gags, as even just the reminder that I didn't need to take absolutely everything so terribly seriously was helpful to me.

Now — of course I am not recommending that you go around wrecking other people's projects or being immature or trying to work while impaired. That would be ridiculous. (Possibly hilarious, but ridiculous nonetheless.) But I do think there's wisdom in Stephen's advice if we think a bit more broadly — and less literally — about these ideas. Let me explain…

### Is Your Desire to Do Well Getting in the Way of Your Doing Well?

Let's think about that for a moment. In what way might your desire to do well (aka not fuck shit up) be getting in the way of you doing better?

Your desire to do well (not fuck shit up) could mean that you hold yourself back.

Think of all the things you don't say, the opinions you don't share. The writing you don't publish. The chances or risks you don't take.

Maybe you:

- think your work has to be as good as your teachers'.
- let fear of failure win.
- just don't ever start.
- worry, "What if I'm wrong?"
- do a ton of research to make sure you don't mess up, then get too intimidated to begin.
- procrastinate because you worry you might not do it right.
- grew up with people who criticized, so you still don't dare try.

Do you end up driving with one foot on the gas and one foot on the brake because you are afraid to fail in some way? Or do you overdo so you can't be accused of slacking? Maybe you give up too soon? Or just stay stuck in a rut because it feels "safer"?

### What Would It Mean for You to "Fuck Shit Up"?

Maybe you could just dive in, without a lot of overthinking, and see what happens?

Maybe you could sort of half-ass it, and see if "getting a C" is good enough?

Perhaps you could ignore some of the dumber institutional rules at play?

I appreciate having high standards, but perhaps it's not essential that they be quite so high, you know? Consider where doing the bare minimum might be fine. Or just giving yourself permission to not be quite so careful?

For example, I used to hesitate to give my designer the specs for a new worksheet, because I felt like I had to give her something that was beautifully laid out and perfectly clear. She finally let me know that I could just rough something out on a legal pad, take a picture of it, send it over, and she could take the project from there. The first time I did this, it felt like I was "fucking shit up" because I was sharing something so halfbaked, but then I realized that giving her more creative freedom was leading to a better end result. Plus, I was no longer spending time doing unnecessary work that stressed me out.

### And What about "Whine and Cry"?

What could "whine and cry" mean for you? Perhaps it's an opportunity to ask — clearly and without apology — for what you want.
Or to just *take* what you want without asking. (Gasp! I know, riiiiight?)
Or perhaps it means admitting to yourself how tired you actually are.
Maybe you could quit being such a good sport all the time, and instead have a frank conversation about what is, and is not, working for you.

For those of us who make a near religion out of never complaining, the simple, daring act of asking, taking, or admitting might feel like "whining and crying," but let me assure you — it's not. Your honesty — no matter how uncomfortable it feels in the moment — helps the rest of us and gives us all a chance to figure out a better way.

### *What Could "Show Up Stoned" Mean for You?*

"Show up stoned" is my favorite because it makes me think of a lot of fun ways to "be," other than afraid.

For example, if I were stoned, I might just take everything as it comes and not be spinning out by trying to think so far ahead.

I might not feel disgruntled when others are doing things differently than I would do them. (Since we all know that judging people according to our own standards is an express elevator to hell.)

Maybe I could allow myself to go with the flow? Or to get absorbed in what's happening without worrying about how I might appear — without self-judgment?

## 15-Minute Experiment

Make a 90-second doodle of how it feels to be so afraid to fail.

Here are some images others have drawn, to inspire you:

- An oversized eyeball, always watching and evaluating
- Sitting in the dark in the very last row of a theater, being totally unnoticed
- An ever-tightening spiral
- Peeking out from under the covers, afraid to emerge
- Storm clouds and heavy, low fog
- Electricity coming out of my brain and a paper bag over my head
- Hiding under a table
- I'm very small, sitting alone in the corner and watching others walk away together toward sunshine, unaware of me

- Hands and mind going in all potential directions, me hoping one of them is right
- In a cave with bars across the entrance and a raging river out front

Can you feel the constriction? The fear? The invisibility?

Next, doodle yourself in a contented, even joyful state of fucking shit up, whining and crying, and/or showing up stoned.

Here are a few examples from my clients:

- Me with a Buddha smile
- Me totally relaxed and laughing; others around me relaxed and happy, too, surrounded by sunflowers
- Me springing from bed — flinging covers aside, ready to take on whatever comes
- Me scribbling away — suddenly prolific
- Me sitting under a tree holding a bouquet of flowers while a bunch of little stick figures are running around holding clipboards
- Me and my favorite people gathered around the table, having fun — not hiding
- Two stick figures greeting each other, shaking hands — and a dotted line connecting their hearts

## What If...

What if you traded perfectionism for poetry?

# 10

# Intermezzo: Ode to the Busy Bee

I see you
Making life easier for everyone else.
The way you are patient with the clerk
Pick up yet another errant sock
Get another mostly homemade meal on the table
Plus extra in a Tupperware for the ailing neighbor.

*Busy* is a word you left behind long ago
Because it implies that there is a world — or a day —
In which you are not busy.

In every moment you are working, planning —
Juggling —
Giving your warmhearted attention to this issue and the next
To this needy person and the next.

And it seems like being strong and capable is
Its own punishment
Every problem a sharp-toothed hydra, growing two heads for
Each one you think you've handled.

Everyone turns to you.
Every problem is yours to solve.

And you still feel as though maybe you are not
Doing enough.

The painful fear of failing is
Worse than the fatigue

So you keep going.

Luckily, you have an excellent sense of humor
And a love of long walks
And three close friends on speed dial.

And you are excellent at counting your blessings.

Blessed are those in back-to-back meetings, for theirs is the
    patience of mountains.
Blessed are those who are annoyed by willful ignorance, for
    theirs is a righteous fury.
Blessed are the uncomplaining, for theirs is a peaceful
    surrender to the inanities of the world.
Blessed are those who hunger and thirst for carbs and wine,
    for they shall be comforted.

Blessed are those who dance in the kitchen
Make time for family game night
Say "I love you" at every single opportunity
Ignoring the eye rolls of the young ones
As they go out of their way to make an
Ordinary moment
A memory.

Because it is the memories that matter.
A legacy of moonlight on mown grass
And a quick hug.

You are indeed as busy as a bee — the Queen Bee —

Sensitive to the hum of the whole hive
Filled with sweetness and good medicine

The center of the whole ecosystem, really.

The center of the benevolent hum.

# 11

# Your Path of Resistance

We all have our favorite ways of working. And we also all have our favorite ways of staying stuck. See which one of these scenarios resonates for you:

You have an idea that you're excited about, and then you...

- decide it's too hard, expensive, or complicated, and quit.
- get stuck on the tech — like you realize you might need a new computer, or you can't figure out the software, or there's some new appliance you need to learn — and it all feels too annoying to keep going, so you quit.
- mention it to the one person who says the exact right thing to discourage you, and you quit.
- get distracted by another idea, and even though you promise yourself you'll get back to it, you've effectively quit.
- find another obligation to be more important, so you quit.
- watch your inner rebel sloooowly cross their arms... and you know: you are never going to be able to convince yourself to take further action, so you quit.
- remember all the other projects you've started and not completed, get discouraged, and quit.
- spend a ton of money on equipment or training, and then quit.

- call 57 people to ask their opinion about this idea instead of taking meaningful action and then, confused by too much hypothetical feedback, you quit.
- do hours of research, and then quit.
- decide that it feels like everyone else is already doing this, and quit.
- determine there's no money in it, and quit.
- remember your friend who's already succeeded at this, and quit.
- rush into it, get two-thirds of the way through, then quit.
- get 99 percent of the way done, then quit.
- finish it — YAY! You didn't quit! Then stick it in a closet forever.

What does your pattern of quitting or staying stuck tell you? What do you notice?

## 15-Minute Experiment

Spend 15 minutes doodling, drawing, journaling about, or otherwise processing the results of this inquiry.

## What If...

What if having the courage of your convictions meant that you never, ever, ever missed one of your 15-minute sessions?

# 12

# The Perfect Version

The perfect version of your project — the one that exists only in your head — is almost useless. It's right up there with comparing yourself to how you looked 20 years ago, or thinking how great your spouse would be if only they were different.

And yet there is a desire to cling to the perfect version, isn't there?

In the perfect version inside your head, there is no criticism by others, no wasted effort from you, nothing to dislike. You know why? Because there's nothing actually happening. Just your imagination, picturing a perfect world.

You may have been taught to believe thoughts like:

> "If it can't be perfect, why even try?"
> "If I can't be the best, I don't want to begin."
> "I need to be able to think the whole thing through in advance before I can start."
> "If I start and it's not good enough, I'll just get frustrated and quit."
> "I'm sure someone else has already done this better than I could."

These thoughts are bullshit.

They are actually bullshit with extra bullshittiness, because there is the faint whiff of superiority in them, isn't there? This tone that you and you alone know what "good" or "good enough" is. The idea that you are the ultimate arbiter of taste, and that you are somehow in control of how things roll out in your life.

So let's take them apart:

### "If it can't be perfect, why even try?"

There is a belief here that "perfect" is not only a thing, but a desirable thing. In fact, the imperfections are often what make things lovable. Do you love your best friend because they are perfect? Is your favorite book or movie or song perfect? Of course not. In fact, some of my favorite people, books, films, and songs are wildly imperfect. Yours, too, I bet.

The "why even try?" part says, "I'd rather stay up here in the tower, swathed in self-satisfaction because I don't have to worry about getting grubby and dirty down there in the mud." Which must be one of the hollowest victories of all.

### "If I can't be the best, I don't want to begin."

This is very similar to the thought above, but with some added bullshitty-tastic-ness about how there's some kind of competition going on and you need to be winning it. And your way of winning is to disqualify yourself in the first place.

### "I need to be able to think the whole thing through in advance before I can start."

Now, this almost sounds rational. But it's not. It's crazy. Because you can't know what you don't know. Most of what you need to know about your project you will discover in the doing of it.

It's not really possible to think a project all the way through, especially one that is supposed to be life-enhancing, or even life-changing. In fact, figuring it out as you go is half the fun.

The other half of the fun is evolving as you learn from this project. And if you ask me, becoming yourself — discovering who you are as you do hard things — is the most fun possible.

*"If I start and it's not good enough, I'll just get frustrated and quit."*

When you were little, we would have called that "throwing a tantrum." While I sympathize with the frustration of not being able to execute at the level of your vision, I believe you are emotionally mature enough to persevere. And again, sometimes "not good enough" is actually fine, or even delightful.

*"I'm sure someone else has already done this better than I could."*

Oh, I'm absolutely positive that's true. I also know that it doesn't matter. It doesn't matter because of some of the dynamics we've already discussed: that "perfect" or even "better" isn't possible or even preferable, and that the person you'll become as you do this project — no matter how poorly you perform — is worth the investment of time and energy.

The other reason is from one of my favorite sayings:

It's all been done before…but not by you.

I'm sure you've had the experience of hearing something a thousand times, and then suddenly someone says it in a way that is so illuminating that suddenly you get it. Sometimes people need to hear the truth from you and no one else.

We never tire of great stories or good jokes or excellent recipes, and frankly, we want yours shared in the world. Sooner rather than later, please.

## The Alchemy of Effort

The final problem I see with allowing your perfectionism to keep your idea locked inside your head is that, while it stays hermetically sealed, it can't have an impact on me or on the world.

So you never get to experience the Alchemy of Effort.

Here's how the Alchemy of Effort works:

You put some effort into making something, and you are changed by making the effort.

Then you let it out of the house, and you are changed by the effort of releasing it into the world.

I see or encounter the effects of your effort — I read your book, I see the boat you built, I admire your hand-painted shoes — and then I am changed. The work means something different to me than it does to you, so the meaning of the work itself is changed.

Let's say that now I thank you for your effort and tell you what it meant to me. Now you are changed, the work is changed, I am changed, and now you are changed again. And this looping figure eight that represents the energetic transfer of effort is what I like to call the Alchemy of Effort. Because it grows so far beyond the sum of its parts and can effect change throughout time and space, it's a form of magic.

You never know how the things you do will affect the world. And the more you make and participate and laugh and fail and create and fail again and laugh again, the more magic you will make.

So are you willing to believe that some of these words could be more important than *perfect*?

| | |
|---|---|
| magic | weird |
| authentic | profitable |
| heartfelt | current |
| wild | correct |
| real | needed |
| expressive | sexy |
| unusual | delicious |
| handmade | life-affirming |
| naive | inspiring |
| compelling | energetic |
| spectacular | sophisticated |
| done | luscious |
| graceful | fun |
| thoughtful | luxurious |
| peaceful | noisy |
| prayerful | creative |
| delightful | daring |
| hilarious | delicate |
| genius | |

## 15-Minute Experiment

Reflect on which words you could choose to focus on — other than *perfect* — and perhaps add to this list.

## *What If...*

What if you doing your meaningful work today inspired someone else to do theirs? And what if that person's work inspired two more people? And so on...and so on. What if you were able to initiate a global avalanche of good-feeling productivity?

# 13

# Turn Your Weaknesses into Strengths

The immortal classic ballad "Send In the Clowns" was written when the Broadway show *A Little Night Music* was in rehearsals. Hal Prince, the director, felt like the character of Desirée needed a solo, and Stephen Sondheim, the composer and lyricist, agreed. The role of Desirée was being played by the marvelous British actress Glynis Johns. As it happens, Johns had a very light, breathy voice and not much range. She couldn't really sustain a long note or a long phrase, nor perform the big swoops of melody that can make solos so compelling. So Sondheim went the opposite way and turned her shortcomings into strengths. Rather than an oversized, chest-thumping, melodic roller coaster, the song is delicate, rueful, and quiet. The lyrics are a series of short questions, many of them ironic, leaving a lot of room for the true romantic heart of the character, and by extension the show itself, to be felt.

I learned this trick of turning weaknesses into strengths from another great comic mind: the writer, performer, and director Ron West. Ron has been a director with the Second City theatre for over 30 years, and a recent reviewer said that he was "inarguably among the top two or three most influential directors and performers" of that venerable institution.

I know him because I was married to him, so I can say definitively that he's a great guy and hella funny.*

Ron West has made an art form out of turning performers' weaknesses into strengths. If an actor can't dance, he'll create a bit of choreography that highlights the actor flailing around, completely out of step with everyone else, and it's hilarious. I've seen him turn apparent disadvantages — such as a strong accent, an inability to remember blocking, and extreme shyness — into indelible comic moments.

One time, we were doing a show together, and one of the actors — let's call him "Actor" — was almost undirectable. Every time Ron would make a suggestion to Actor, Actor would immediately disagree and suggest the opposite. It didn't take Ron long to turn things around: he simply started giving Actor directions that were the exact opposite of what Ron wanted.

Ron would say, "So, Actor, I'd like you to turn away from Other Actor, face out, and say this line directly to the audience." "No!" Actor would reply. "I think I should look right into Other Actor's eyes and say it just to her."

"Oh, OK," Ron would say, having just gotten exactly what he wanted.

---

\* Are you now wondering how many husbands I've had? Just the two. Plus Luke, who, after 12 years together, I referred to as my "husband-ish" because we were married-ish. When we moved in together, I asked him for a ring, partly because I like jewelry and partly because I didn't want to walk around looking like I was available when I wasn't. When he gave me the ring, he looked deeply into my eyes and said, "I guess I should ask you, darling — will you not marry me?" I kissed him and said, "I would love to not marry you. I will not marry you every single day." #trueromance

Luke and I recently parted ways in the same easy, honest, kind, and peaceful way that we began. So I guess now I'm happily divorced-ish.

If you have a rebellious person in your family, or on your team, you may want to employ this method. It's not just reverse psychology — it's reverse everything. Used stealthily, it can work miracles.

## No Gift for Plot

Some years ago, I was asked to write the book to a musical. (The "book" is the script part of a musical — the talking parts that come between the songs.) Now, I had written nonfiction books, plus a solo performance piece and a ton of sketch comedy, but I had never succeeded at writing a full-length play or screenplay. Lawd knows I tried. But while characters and dialogue come easily, it turns out I have absolutely no gift for plot. I can dream up the vague outline for a story, but when I start thinking about the action of the story, I get stuck. "Maybe the hero meets the villain in a hallway? No — an elevator. Are they wearing sweats? Tuxedos?" I stall out almost immediately.

I almost said no. But this show was the brainchild of my best friend, the songwriter, producer, and now successful novelist Phil Swann, and the legendary Al Kasha. Al won Academy Awards for the songs "The Morning After" and "We May Never Love Like This Again," plus more awards for creating the music for the film *Pete's Dragon* and the score for *Seven Brides for Seven Brothers* on Broadway. Al was a legend and the kindest man I ever met.* Phil wanted me to partner with him and Al to write this two-person musical. It was to be set in Hollywood in 1949 to 1952, and it was called *In a Booth at*

---

\* Fun sidenote, one of Phil Swann's other frequent collaborators is the aforementioned Ron West, and Luke has worked as an arranger and orchestrator with all of us. We're all very chummy.

*Chasen's: The Real-Life Hollywood Romance of Ron and Nancy Reagan.*

Although I was afraid that working on this show might revoke my card-carrying status as a *Free to Be You and Me*, tie-dyed-in-the-wool liberal, I agreed to try. After all, this show took place long before Ron and Nancy were in any way political — they were both working actors in Hollywood at the time. I dove into a ton of research, mostly relying on primary sources, and started to create the outline of the show.

"Sam," Phil warned me one day, "you should know that you have the worst job in musical theater. You have to write all the boring stuff, and the minute something interesting happens, the characters will start singing. Once we open, if the show is a flop, they will blame the book. If the show is a success, they will ignore the book completely. You can't win." I decided that sounded more like a challenge than a threat, and I persevered.

I realized I had lucked into the *one* theater writing gig I could actually pull off — short, dialogue-heavy scenes featuring a lot of flirting, with absolutely no need to create a plot. We all know the plot: they meet, they date, they fall in love, they almost break up, then they get engaged and live happily ever after, eventually becoming the influential figures we know them as today.

I loved working on the script and found the constraints very freeing. Luckily, the show found a wonderful producer and had a wildly successful run in Los Angeles in late 2018. My favorite moment was when Michael Reagan (Ronald's son) and some other members of the Reagan family came and were amazed at how spot-on the show was. They wondered how I had known such intimate things about Ron and Nancy's relationship, and I explained that I had done a bunch of research and then used my writerly talents and…guessed. The rave reviews even praised the "lively dialogue."*

## *Please* And *Your* Buts

Finally, I find this weaknesses-into-strengths thing can work wonders when people are using their weaknesses as an excuse for not following their dreams.

> "I want to start a side hustle, but I've never been an entrepreneur before…"
> "I want to be a health coach, but I'm 100 pounds overweight…"
> "I want to write a book, but I'm 85 years old…"

Here's the trick: turn the *but* into an *and*, and make it the highlight of your story.

> "I started a side hustle, *and* I've never been an entrepreneur before."
> "I'm a health coach, *and* I'm overweight."
> "I wrote a book, *and* I'm 85 years old."

You are perfectly designed to do what you want to do. You may not do it the same way everyone else might, which is a good thing. You may not do it the "right" way, which is also a good thing.

Suddenly, your shortcomings are not a bug, they're a feature.

---

\*    So there, Phil.

    Curious about the future of this show? Me, too. We were prepping for a national tour when the pandemic hit, and we had to go dark for a few years. But we've got our fingers crossed. Stay tuned. It really is a delightfully romantic little valentine of a show, if I do say so myself. You can see more about it at InABoothAtChasens.com

## 15-Minute Experiment

Reflect on a few examples from your own life where you or someone else succeeded despite the odds being against them. What are some of your perceived weaknesses that you've turned into strengths?

## What If...

What if you turned your perceived shortcomings into strengths? So if your shortcoming is being stuck with a small budget, what if you made austerity a key part of your plan? Or if your shortcoming is that you are "too" old, tall, or weird, what if you made age, height, or oddness the main feature of your marketing, your flirty profile, or your story?

# 14

# Noticing the Critical Voices

You know what I notice? I notice how much we notice what we notice.

In other words, I notice that *all* we notice is that which we are prepared or programmed to notice. And the rest of it often slips right by us.

For example, because I'm an actor, every TV show, movie, or commercial I watch, I am noticing the actors. I tend to remember their names and notice what else they've been in. This drives my niece crazy. We'll be watching a show, and suddenly I'll pipe up with, "Oh, look — there's That Actor named XYZ! I love them. I knew them a little bit because we did a show together in LA back in the '90s, and I loved them when they did the guest spot on that other sitcom…"

"STOP!" my darling niece will holler. "You're ruining it!"

By which she means, she wants to just accept the actor as the character they are playing. She likes to keep the illusion of the show intact. She doesn't want to consider that these are real people. And unless the actor is one of her all-time favorites, she genuinely doesn't notice or remember them. She hasn't trained herself to notice actors as people, separate from their performances.

I have a lot of professional musician friends, and I'm always surprised and a bit amazed when we're at the local diner and suddenly, midpancake, someone says, "Oh, I love the arrangement of this song," and the rest of the musicians chime in about how they do or don't like it, too, especially because of the horn arrangement in the bridge, etc. And I'm sitting there like a lump thinking, "Ummmmm…is there music playing? Oh — I guess now that you mention it, there is."

My musician friends are interested in music, and trained in music, so they are going to notice it right away, and keep noticing it, even when it's just background noise to you and me.

Choreographers notice movement. Architects notice structures. Engineers notice problem-solving. People in adorably themed appliquéd sweaters recognize other people in adorably themed appliquéd sweaters.*

In addition to noticing things that fall inside our sphere of interest and expertise, we also tend to notice any negative events and feedback, because we are slightly negatively programmed. After all, from a survival point of view, it is more important that we remember the dangerous ledge, the poisonous plant, and the disapproved-of behavior than that we remember what's generally safe and approved of.

This is why when you do something, and 99 people love it and tell you how great it is, but then one person says something a teensy bit critical, that criticism is all you hear. That's not low self-esteem. That's your survival mechanism kicking in.

---

* Some of those sweaters, and the people who wear them, are known as Quackers, and apparently, when Quackers travel, they often wear their glitzed-up sweaters on purpose, so that other Quackers, or anyone in need, can find them. Just in case you need someone to ask directions of, or otherwise need help, you can, in theory, trust that a Quacker will be nice. Isn't that sweet?

## 15-Minute Experiment

Let's take steps to override your slightly negative programming: Spend 15 minutes writing down 10 nice pieces of positive feedback you've received. And then do it again tomorrow. Do this for 90 days straight, and I bet your impostor syndrome will disappear forever.

## *What If...*

What if you were as kind to yourself as you are to everyone else?

# 15

# Spotlight Syndrome

The spotlight effect is the illusion we have when we think people are noticing us, but they're not. It's a very common psychological phenomenon. For example, you may stumble over your words in a conversation and instantly think, "Oh no — now everyone must think I'm a total loser," when, in fact, they probably didn't notice at all, or if they did notice, they didn't think much about it one way or the other.

Mostly because they are way too busy being burdened by their own spotlight effect.

When you are super self-conscious, the simple act of "putting yourself out there" can be absolutely excruciating. Sometimes, your self-consciousness can be so consuming that it affects your entire perception of reality.

One time, I traveled to Arizona to deliver a corporate keynote. My driver from the airport was pretty quiet, and I was tired from the flight, so we didn't talk much on our way to the hotel. Now, the hotel I was staying at is known for hiring very young, very enthusiastic people to work the front desk. Which is a smart move on the hotel's part, because it means they are giving younger people an opportunity to learn the hospitality business, thus cultivating future leaders, but it's a starter job, so they don't have to pay these young folks much, and they get the benefit of giving their brand a fun, wholesome vibe. And I must say, feeling truly welcomed by a jovial hotel staff makes business travel (slightly) more tolerable.

As we pulled up at the entrance to the hotel, the driver and I both got out of the car to get my luggage out of the trunk. I saw for the first time that he was well over six feet tall and weighed maybe 400 pounds. One of the exuberant young people from the hotel came out to welcome us and help with the bag, and he shouted out, "Hey! Fat Man!"

My head snapped up just in time to see the driver stop dead in his tracks. He pivoted, turned to the kid, and in a low, ominous voice said, "What did you say?"

The kid bounced up toward the car like a 20-something Tigger. "I said, 'Hey, Batman!' Because of your T-shirt! That's an awesome T-shirt!"

Indeed, the driver was wearing a Batman T-shirt.

He looked down at his sizable chest. "Oh. Yeah. Batman."

Tigger started chatting about some Batman trivia with the driver, and I scuttled into the hotel lobby, leaving the two of them, my heart slightly broken by the face of the driver, who'd thought he was being so casually insulted, and slightly healed by the innocent charm of Tigger.

How often have you heard an insult when there wasn't one? How often have you felt slighted when no slight was intended? How often have you assumed that someone else's behavior was directed at you, when it wasn't?

What pain have those imagined offenses caused you?

## Stop Firing Yourself

I remember screwing up while performing in a huge improv show. We were playing a sold-out 1,400-seat theater, and we had a number of celebrity guests. I was in the scene that was ending the first act, and I fumbled. Now, fumbling in an improv show is actually sort of a blessing, because since it's being invented as it's being performed, you and the audience are all in on it together, so screwing up can become kind of an in-joke, or even a magical portal to a better scene. But not that day. Not for me, anyway. I made so many missteps while performing that I started to feel as though the air was made out of glue and I was flailing in slow motion. I remember catching the eye of my friend — one of the other performers — and her expression plainly said, "What is the matter with you right now???"

At intermission I went out into the parking lot, sobbing hysterically, because I could not stop the barrage of voices in my head telling me what a giant fucking idiot I was, what a hopeless failure I was, what a ridiculous fool I was for thinking I could ever make it in Hollywood. I felt sure I should be fired on the spot.

The fact that I was — in that very moment — being paid to improvise with celebrities in front of a huge live audience in LA did nothing to scrape my self-esteem off the floor. Finally, I heard the stage manager calling for us to gather for the second act, so I splashed my blotchy face with cold water and tried to slow my breathing. One of the celebrities took one look at me, gave me a quick hug, and said, "You know it's just a show, right? Let's go play."

He had noticed that I was upset. He had not noticed that I performed badly. Or if he had, he was over it. Only I was still rerunning my failure in my head.

I somehow made it through the second act, but I did not go to the after-party, where I might have made some powerful new friends or even just, you know, had fun.*

The shame of my perceived failure haunted me for weeks. Who knows how many fruitful conversations I could have had during that time if I hadn't been busy licking my invisible wounds? How many auditions did I tank during those weeks because I was so afraid of failing that I failed?

It is not important that you show up and be brilliant 100 percent of the time.

It is not important (or even possible) that you never screw up.

It is only important that you keep going.
That you keep showing up.
That you forgive yourself — and others — and keep trying to become more resilient.
It's important that you don't miss moments of your life because you are busy living inside another moment — maybe a moment that never even happened.

I consider myself successful now not because I never screw up — believe me, I screw up often — but because it no longer ruins my inner monologue for days at a time. It's not that my feelings don't get hurt — I'm just as much of a delicate flower as I was in the fourth grade, when one of my classmates kept

---

\* I will say, though, that it's very rare to have fun at a Hollywood party, because all the creative geniuses in Hollywood were the weird kids in school. We were the ones who never went to the dances, or if we did, we stayed firmly against the wall of the gym. Unless we were with a bunch of other theater nerds, and then we might start performing the choreography from *Pippin*. Anyway, much of Hollywood is a bunch of introverts and obsessives, so we're not great at big social occasions.

track of how many days in a row I cried at school.* But these days, my hurt feelings heal a lot more quickly than they used to.

Seek compassion for yourself.

Seek forgiveness for those who you think have wounded you.

Seek resilience so you can keep sharing your wonderful self with the world. Not perfect, not without scars, but still in the game.

Let's play, Batman.

## 15-Minute Experiment

Can you think of a time when you misinterpreted some feedback? When you were waving wildly and then thought someone was ignoring you, when in fact they just couldn't see you? When you were self-critical about something other people didn't even notice? Can you forgive yourself and others for taking things too personally? Can you forgive yourself and others for poor communication? If you are so inclined, perhaps write or say a little blessing to your former self, and also to those who wronged you, intentionally or not.

## What If...

What if every criticism you've ever gotten was intended as a neutral remark, or even a compliment?

---

\* I don't know the actual number, but I'm sure it was a lot. I was a pretty troubled and depressed kid, and in the mid '70s all anybody ever said about that was "She is just soooo sensitive."

# 16

# Stupid Rules

I want to invite you into a new morality.

There may be moments of reading this book when you think: "Wow, this inner-work crap can fuck you up."

You think you've bought a book on time management, or self-improvement, filled with cheerful little tricks and tips that will improve your day-to-day.

And you have. (Well done, you.) But you may notice an undercurrent of quiet revolution in this book.

Something that may upset your well-ordered world.
Something subversive.
Something even...anarchic.

Because if you're stuck in your life, what is keeping you stuck isn't really about what you are or are not doing with your time. It's about what you are thinking and believing about the world.

It's very likely because you have been taught to obey rules that are, for lack of a better term, absolute horseshit. And once you get a line on exactly how much horseshit you've been asked to believe, and how many stupid, oppressive rules you've been playing by, you might get mad.

As many wise women have said before me: The truth will set you free. But first it will piss you off.

## Absolute Horseshit? Or Worthy Principles?

How many of the following statements were you taught? How many do you believe to be true? Most importantly, how has the unquestioned acceptance of them impeded your freedom, self-growth, and happiness?

NOTE: Do not "score" yourself. This is not a *Cosmo* quiz. This is a moment of self-inquiry for you to notice which of these beliefs and commands strike a chord, and which ones may have been exerting invisible control over your decisions. It's not a right-or-wrong thing. All these statements are, or can be, worthy in some instances and not at all valid in others. Just notice which ones resonate for you, and maybe use that realization as an opportunity to examine some of the day-to-day choices you make.

> Grades matter.
> Honor your mother and father.
> Good work will be rewarded.
> If you work hard, you will succeed.
> Don't rock the boat.
> Be likable.
> Good parents sacrifice for their children.
> It's OK that men do less housework.
> You should save stuff like boxes and old ties because you might need them someday.
> It's OK that women do most of the household organizing (birthday parties, filling out school forms, shopping, planning, social arrangements, etc.).
> Hobbies aren't serious or important.
> Wealthy people are shallow.
> Poor people are virtuous.
> Don't sell out.
> Don't be selfish.

Marriage is hard.

Don't get too big for your britches.

It's important to be attractive, and it's worth spending lots of time and money on your physical appearance.

Divorce is a kind of failure.

Save your "good" china, jewelry, and clothes for special occasions.

Poor housekeeping is a sign of a moral failing.*

Be well behaved.

Girls are either pretty or smart.

Boys are either weak or strong.

Fat people are doing something wrong.

It's more important to do stuff for other people than to do your own thing.

Don't be selfish.

Don't think you're so special.

Confessing your feelings makes you weak.

All you need is love. Love conquers all.

How happy is a person supposed to be, really?

It's better to be thin.

Addiction is a kind of failure.

Be productive.

Don't have sex with anyone with whom you are not in a committed relationship.

Definitely don't have sex with strangers.

In the US, overall, it is better to be a white straight man.

---

\*    Did you know that, as near as etymologists can tell, the origin of the word *slut* is "poor housekeeper"? Same root word as *slattern* and *slovenly*. Interesting that I can't think of a word that connects a male person's housekeeping abilities with promiscuous sexual behavior. #themoreyouknow

Finish what's on your plate.

It's important that your home and office are clean and
well organized.

Sales is hard. Sales is sleazy. Sales is manipulative.

Don't toot your own horn.

You should have something to fall back on.

Making money is hard.

Everybody is working for the weekend.

Don't be too provocative.

Get all your work done first, then you can play.

Make sure you're blameless.

Success doing what you love is hard to achieve.

In order to look or appear "professional" you have to
dress in a certain way.

Don't disagree with people. It's rude.

Men are successful; women are nice.

Life is short — grab the good stuff while you can.

It's very important to stay current with the latest hair,
makeup, and fashion trends.*

It's bad to have wrinkles.

Having some feelings? Yeah. Me, too.

---

*   Can you imagine if womenfolk just said no to all beauty procedures and
    processes that most men don't do? Or if they stopped buying all optional
    clothing and all accessories (I'm looking at you, shapewear, hose, and heels)
    that men don't have to buy? Might have a bit of an effect on the econ-
    omy. Might make getting ready for work a much quicker morning routine.
    And then maybe we could open up the beauty and fashion thing *more* for
    the people who are into it — so anyone who really *likes* getting all fancy
    with makeup and clothes could feel comfortable doing so regardless of
    age/gender/size/whatever, without experiencing any backlash — while still
    keeping it optional for those of us who just aren't. I'm one of the latter,
    though I do enjoy a nice red lipstick. So classic.

Mostly, this list makes me want to cry and scream and burn down the patriarchy and possibly burn down the oppressive matriarchy (shame passed down from mother to daughter; a history of some womenfolk not supporting one another). Perhaps one of the reasons that the American feminist movement has never been as successful as it deserves to be is because so many of us (me included) could not figure out a way to be strong and ask for what we wanted while simultaneously remaining "attractive" and "likable."

"But you have to be likable," says the Inner Stupid Rule. "That's the most important thing!"* And I, for one, believed that voice.

## What Will Others Think?

For many of you, this is not your first self-help rodeo — you've already done a lot of work on yourself and your mindset, and you've taken a look at the ways you've been programmed to believe limiting thoughts. But what I've noticed in 20+ years of working with highly intelligent, highly emotionally intelligent, highly creative, and overall completely excellent people is that, even with all the therapy and workshops and personal development, many of us are still heavily invested in behaving like good little schoolchildren.

We are still afraid of what others might think.
We are afraid to speak our mind in public.
We are afraid that others might think we are selfish or weird or both.

So, it is more important to us to be well liked than to risk rocking the boat to make progress in our lives. More important that

---

\* And do we really mean "likable"? Or do we mean "fuckable"? Asking for a friend.

we make brownies for the bake sale than write our novel. More important that we know every detail of our favorite team's statistics than it is to understand what's happening in the internal life of our teenage kid.

What have you sacrificed in the name of being faithful, likable, or prudent? What have you gained from being faithful, likable, or prudent?

## Empathy and Curiosity

Once you get in the habit of questioning your own indoctrinated beliefs from a place of empathy and curiosity, perhaps you might start greeting other people's beliefs with empathy and curiosity.

Next time you find you disagree with someone, you might find yourself saying, "That's interesting — tell me more about why you believe that." And you might keep investigating until you realize that, while you may still disagree, you share a desire to understand the other. And that builds a bridge.

I want you to stop being so reactive to everyone else. I want you to stop being so certain that your judgment about how someone else should be, look, or feel is correct. I want you to approach challenges with good humor and patience and, yes, empathy and curiosity.

And if you're nodding and smiling and feeling slightly saintly right now because you think you already have this one dialed, I invite you to consider how you talk about the political candidate you abhor, or the family member who betrayed you.

See?

Even the wise ones lose their perspective occasionally, so it's worth continuing this work.

## 15-Minute Experiment

1.  Write down five rules that you regularly break, five rules that you would like to break, and five rules that you think deserve to be obeyed. If it feels good, maybe create a story or drawing about you and your rules.
2.  If any of the statements listed above make you blink rapidly and think, "Wait — but that's TRUE!!" then I invite you to spend 15 minutes investigating that particular statement. Write about why it's useful as a brainwashing technique. Maybe make a 90-second doodle about some of the instances in which it is true, and others in which it isn't. In other words, spend 15 minutes finding the subtlety, poetry, nonsense, and humanity in what has, up to now, been an unquestioned bumper sticker for you.

### What If...

What if you only did 14 minutes today? Or pushed it to 16? (In other words: Where is rule-following getting in your way?)

# 17

# Bless Your Life Correct

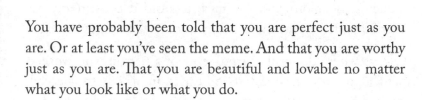

You have probably been told that you are perfect just as you are. Or at least you've seen the meme. And that you are worthy just as you are. That you are beautiful and lovable no matter what you look like or what you do.

But the world doesn't do much to reinforce that idea. And even if it did, some of us are stubborn.

Me. I am stubborn. Maybe you are, too.

No matter how many lessons I get (and give) about self-love, I still can have the feeling that I need to work harder, exercise harder, be more charming, make more money, and be in a constant state of exhaustion in order to justify my existence.

*Busy* is a fabulous narcotic. *Busy* means I am valuable. *Busy* means I am needed and necessary. *Busy* used to be my identity.

And as my friends started to have children — thereby entering a whole new world of "busy" and "exhausted" — I felt it was my obligation to make the most out of every moment. After all, I wasn't consumed by the day-to-day needs of a toddler, so what excuse did I have? I must work. I must prove my value to the world. Then my infertility journey overtook my life (which is a story for another time), and simultaneously, my hunger to prove that I was a worthwhile person overtook my life.

If I couldn't be a mom, I'd better be something important. Otherwise, what good was I? What was my legacy? So I worked as hard as I could to succeed in Hollywood.

Which, aside from soaring moments of pure joy, was another daily exercise in futility, frustration, and impotence. I mean, at least one study shows that the fact that I ever made any money as a union actor — much less did it consistently for over 20 years — puts me in a tiny minority of all performers.

OK, so where does this narrative — of a person who worked hard at one of the hardest industries in which to succeed, worked hard at getting pregnant and couldn't, worked hard at writing books, worked hard at building her own business, and still struggles — leave me?

I'm left assuming that the decisions I have made and the way my life has played out must be correct.

I mean, what happened is what happened. And as far as we know, there is no alternate version of reality.

So we bless it correct. Life has unfolded. Usually not in the way we expected. But just because things are not going the way we planned does not mean they are not going well.

Now, I get a bit tense when people talk about "destiny," or something being "meant to be," because it implies a certain lack of agency. Also, I refuse to believe that any tragedy is pre-arranged by a divine force. The starving children of the world are not starving because of their lack of a positive mental attitude, nor because God doesn't like them.

Sometimes well-meaning people say, "Everything happens for a reason." What I notice is that everything happens. And I notice that we get to decide what the reason is.

So maybe we could say, "Everything that happens is an opportunity for you to gain a greater understanding of the mysteries of life" instead.

And as long as I'm up here on my soapbox, I also want to take issue with the concept of "manifesting" things and "attracting" things. Partly because there is a strong whiff of "blame the victim" going on here. If you claim to be able to manifest things with your amazing mind power, then you are implying that anyone who cannot make their desires come true just isn't doing it right.

The part that I think is true about the idea of manifesting is that one of the things your brain is best at is this: finding what you tell it to look for. (And that *is* an amazing mind power.) So if you are actively looking for a nice, shaded, free parking space, you have a better chance of finding one. And if you are looking for evidence that you are loved, you will find that, too.

Similarly, if you are seeking evidence that you are unemployable, or that the world is against you, or that people from other cultures are out to ruin your way of life, you will find that, too.

## The Stories We Tell

So I could tell myself the story that all those years in Hollywood were wasted, or I could tell myself that I was reasonably successful in a highly competitive field.

I could tell myself that not being able to have children makes me a failure, or I could take it as a lesson in grace and learning to live peacefully with that which is outside my control.

These past few years I've been unwell — almost bedbound. I could tell myself that I've lost nearly two years to illness, or I could use it to learn something about slowing down, accepting help, and finding peace within.

This is how you live a life without regrets: not by never making mistakes, and not by having everything work out the way you expect, but rather by asking yourself, "What about this situation is teaching me something valuable?"

And again, I notice that there is only one version of my life. So it must, by default, be the correct one.

Can you see that about your life? That the way it is…is the only way it could be — because it's what is?

You cannot fuck up your life.
You cannot fail.
You cannot make "wrong" choices.

You can only make the choices you make. And those choices must be correct, because those choices are what happened and what brought you to today. The steps on your path are yours to own.

Let's agree to have no regrets, shall we?

In a study of hospice patients, nearly all of them confided that overall, their biggest regret was, "I wish I'd had the courage to live a life true to myself, not the life others expected of me."

I'd rather live a life filled with missteps, mistakes, wrong turns, and full-on belly flops that I chose for myself than live in between the narrow lines of someone else's choices.

I mean, when I am long gone, I want my niece and nephew to be telling their children, "Wow — your great-auntie Sam was a woman in love with life. She always noticed the color of the sky and the stages of the moon. She swam in every body of water she could find, read all the books, and wrote a lot. She looked for the good in people and situations, and she mostly didn't complain. She wept and ate and laughed with the joy of a person who knows that while love is eternal, life is fleeting."

I mean, what's the alternative? A memorial gathering in which your friends and family say things like:

> "Her tile grout was always really clean."
> "He never rocked the boat. Ever."
> "She always obeyed the rules and never pissed anyone off."
> "He was exactly the person his parents always hoped he would be."
> "They were always really, really, really, really, really BUSY."

Nope. We're not here to do everything perfectly. We're here to do everything imperfectly and then gather that whole mess up in our arms, give it a hug, and discover that in fact, this bundle of mud and glitter is perfect after all, because it is ours, and it is us.

## 15-Minute Experiment

What might the benefits of some of your least-favorite life experiences be? This experiment is not intended to whitewash them, or to diminish their awfulness, but rather to rebalance the scales a bit. After all, they did happen, and now you have the power to imbue what happened with meaning. Make some 90-second doodles about it, or maybe create a 10-line story in which you are the brave hero.

## What If…

What if you forgave everyone everything? Including yourself, please.

# 18

# The Question You're Not Asking

Imagine that we are in a medium-size classroom — the Get It Done lab — together. The room is filled with people like you who want to get something done.

First of all, where are you sitting? Front row? Back row? Middle center?*

Now, imagine that the teacher (you can imagine it's me, or someone else — whoever you like) says, "OK — we've been talking about ideas and Zones of Creative Genius. Who has a question for me?"

And there is silence. No one, apparently, has a question. Teacher is waiting expectantly. Silence grows. Now — and this is very important — what are you thinking in this silence?

Common thoughts might be:

> "I don't really have a question."
> "I don't want to take up her time."
> "I'm all good."

---

* If it were me, I'd probably be in the far back corner, due to years of "tall people go to the back" training (I'm nearly six feet) and because I like to be able to see all the people in the room, even if it's from the back. Also, preferably near a door, since I'm ridiculously shy, and if my social anxiety kicks up, I might need to make a speedy exit.

"I'll let someone else go first."

"Why is it so quiet? Oh! Did I miss something?"

"I didn't know we were supposed to prepare a question."

"I wish I could think of a good question."

Please take a moment and write down the exact wording of the phrase in your head as you are busy *not* asking the teacher a question.

Here's the big reveal: the reason you are not asking a question is the exact same reason you get stuck.

Consider:

- Do you silence your inner questioning?
- Do you fear taking up space and time?
- Is it important that you appear entirely competent or self-sufficient?
- Do you put yourself at the back of the line?
- Do you space out and miss cues?
- Do you feel like life is one big pop quiz?
- Do you often hold yourself to an impossibly high standard, even when there's nothing at stake?

If this particular imaginary situation is not bringing up a big moment of illumination for you, I want you to make a mental note for yourself to see if there are any other normal, everyday interactions that might reveal a self-limiting thought pattern. For example, I have never once accepted the grocery bagger's offer to help me out to my car. Even when I had a broken leg. Which is just silly. So the real question is this: Where does my reflexive answer of "No thanks, I got it" get in the way in other areas of my life? What would happen if I accepted offers of help, even if I didn't "need" it?*

Take notice of your insights here, and see if anything else bubbles up for you in the next day or so.

You never know where a bubble might take you.

## 15-Minute Experiment

Reflect on when and how you silence yourself. What were you taught as a kid about asking questions? What do you think might happen if you ask a "dumb" question? Why does silence feel safe? Feel free to write about this, or maybe just mull it over. You can also draw, doodle, make up a little song, create a GIF — whatever appeals to you.

## What If...

What if you took a breath and counted to five before you spoke the question that's in your mind or the truth that's in your heart?

---

\*     I sometimes refer to this as "self-sufficiency disorder," and I notice it afflicts many of us, including eldest siblings, tall people, smart people, emotionally complex people (who might actually like some help, but honestly it's all just too much to explain, right?), and those of us with elaborate homesteader fantasies.

# 19

# Motivation and Rewards

Once I was at a long, delicious dinner party with a bunch of friends. These friends included several award-winning screenwriters, some TV writers (one of whom also wrote books), a lead actor on a TV series, and a photographer. Smart, artsy bunch. And over the course of the evening, someone said, "What's the one thing you could say to any man, anywhere, anytime, that would make him get up and follow you out of the room?"*

"Free blow jobs?" guessed one person.

"But that wouldn't work if they were celibate," countered another.

"How about: I'll give you a million bucks if you come with me right now?"

"Maybe. But what if they are already a billionaire?"

We threw around a few other ideas, and finally our smartest friend came up with a hilarious answer: "Hey, me and some guys are busting up some stuff outside...then we're going to blow it up."

---

\* This was in the early 2000s, when subtleties like "cisgender" and "male" vs. "male-presenting" vs. "masculine" were not part of daily conversation, so please forgive our broad strokes for the sake of the story.

We all laughed and agreed that none of us knew a person who identified as male who would ignore that invitation (and that quite a few womenfolk wouldn't, either).

Then we launched into a long and convoluted conversation that lasted through several more bottles of wine about what a person might be able to say to any woman that would cause her to follow them out of the room, no matter who she was.

Our best result was: "Your best friend is outside, and they need your advice."

Not only was it a very amusing conversation, but we ended up with a pretty tried-and-true *ism* about how some folks are more interested in action and others are more interested in relationships.

People have different motivations, different expectations of story, and different ways of communicating. And the more closely you can pay attention to your own — and others' — the easier it will be to succeed.

## 15-Minute Experiment

Write down the names of five people you work or live with and what you suspect motivates them. What communication styles do they seem to prefer? What invitation would be irresistible to them?

And what about you? What are your preferred motivations, communication styles, and rewards?

Find a way to reality-check your assumption by, say, asking them directly. Or become a spy for love and observe them closely. The more you understand their inner workings, the more you will have a leg up with your coworkers, friends, and family, and you may also discover some new ways to teach people to interact with you more effectively.

## What If...

What if your gift for nuance was helpful today?

# 20

# Does It Hurt?

Once I was in a brutal workout class. We were asked to do this reverse-bear-crawl thing, and it was awful. I was sweating and red-faced almost immediately. The younger people in the class (which was pretty much everyone) seemed not to have much of a problem with this move, but I was going slowly and losing steam with each lurching motion. As the younger people were nimbly, bearishly going along, I felt old and bulky and dumb. I was frustrated. Tears started to fall down my sweaty face.

I had two thoughts:

> Thought One: You could just stand up, get in your car, and go home. I mean, you are paying them to be here. You don't have to do this. Take it easy for once, why don't you?
>
> Thought Two: If you quit this, you will be missing out. You can go slow. You can do this poorly. But you must not quit. You deserve to know if you can see this through.

These two thoughts were battling it out in my head when the trainer came over and took in my distressed expression. "Does it hurt?" she asked, "Or is it just hard?"

Does it hurt?
Or is it just hard?

I looked up at her from my awkward backwards-bear position.

"It's just hard," I said.

"Good." she said.

And she walked away.

I think about this story often, especially when I, or one of my clients, want to give up on something.

Because if it hurts, then you should stop and get help. If it hurts, that pain is an important signal that ought not to be ignored.

But if it's just hard...well, perhaps, in the immortal words of Tom Hanks as Coach Jimmy Dugan in *A League of Their Own*, "It's supposed to be hard. If it wasn't hard, everyone would do it. The hard is what makes it great."

You can do hard things.
You can do easy things, too.

But the hard is what makes you great.

## 15-Minute Experiment

Make some notes about some hard things you've done in your life. I bet you've even done some things that other people thought were impossible. What are the qualities that helped you see it through? Is there something you're thinking of giving up on? Does it hurt? Or is it just hard?

## What If...

What if you acknowledged the depth and breadth of your personal power?

# 21

# *Overwhelmed* Really Means...

Lack of precision in your vocabulary is costing you more than you know.

As it happens, I am a big fan of using all my SAT words whenever possible, but you don't need to be a word nerd to reap the benefits of better languaging.

There are some words that have come to mean too many things, and *overwhelmed* is one of them.

After all, there's a big difference between feeling overwhelmed because you are "drowning in busywork" vs. "furious with a co-worker" vs. "annoyed by the smell coming from the kitchen."

### Alternate Definitions of *Overwhelmed*

I conducted an informal poll on what people meant (or how they felt) when they used the word *overwhelmed*, and I found the responses fascinating:

aggrieved

annoyed

anxious

barely contained fury

bored

broke

broken

bummed out

burdened

buried

busted

can't breathe

can't catch a break

can't have even a moment to

    myself

confused

congested
crowded
decision fatigued
deluged
dissatisfied
don't know where to begin
    because everything is
    calling at the same time
don't speak the language
drowning
dysregulated
envious
everything coming at me
    with equal intensity
exhausted
feeling like I'm not smart
    enough to get what I
    want
feeling out of control
flooded
frozen
fucking furious
furious
haggard
heartbroken
lacking basics
like I'm being pecked to
    death by ducks
like others are determining
    my priorities
marginalized
new rules and no orientation
    session
no free moment in my mind

nothing good to look
    forward to
oppressed
out of control
overcome
oversaturated
paralyzed
powerless
resentful
resistant
restless
short of oxygen
six arms short of an octopus
sleepy
so many things I "should"
    do and none of which I
    want to do
stifled
stuck
swallowed up
swamped
swimming against the tide in
    water too deep
too many feelings
too much to do and not
    enough resources to do it
too-tight shoes
unable to focus
unappreciated
underappreciated
unfit
unsupported

## Underlying Causes of Overwhelm

Read through these and see if any ring a bell about your feelings of overwhelm:

- Are you considering an idea with too many unknowns? But you don't do any research — you just stay paralyzed?
- Are you considering an idea with too many variables? But you don't try to simplify or take smaller, incremental steps — you just spin?
- Have you convinced yourself that your idea might cause other people discomfort and therefore should be rejected? Except that it still won't leave you alone?
- Have you outgrown your current circumstances, but you feel afraid to move on?
- Are you considering an idea that would be easier to deal with if it were ten times smaller? For example: you want to write a book, but that freaks you out, so maybe you could just write a social media post instead, and see how that goes?
- Or perhaps you feel overwhelmed because you are actually underwhelmed, and your idea (or your life) is boring the bejeezus out of you, so maybe it's time to make your idea ten times bigger?
- Do you need to have a hard conversation with someone?
- Are you feeling bored and you need a new challenge?
- Do you have a confession to make?
- Do you have a friend who's not acting like a good friend just now?

When you are able to articulate what's actually going on with you, you can communicate it — most importantly to yourself, but then also to others. Once you can say clearly what it is that's really bothering you, and what, exactly, you are looking for, it becomes a lot easier for you to take steps to help yourself and a lot easier for other people to help you.

## 15-Minute Experiment

Find one time-consuming and nonmandatory recurring item in your routine and eliminate it permanently.

### What If...

What if there was plenty of time in the day?

## 22

# Everyone Is Always Doing Their Best

Everyone is always doing the best they can with the information they have at the time. You have always done your best, given the information you had at the time. You cannot blame someone for not knowing better than they do.

When your child screams, "I HATE YOU!" you forgive them, right? Even though you may feel that your kid is being an ungrateful little horror show, and — more to the point — your feelings may be hurt, you forgive them. You work hard to not yell back. You take a deep breath and understand that this kid is in the grip of a profound frustration and that it will pass.

Everyone is that kid. You are that kid. I am that kid.

I can't tell you how many times I've seen a kid throwing a back-arching tantrum in the grocery store and thought, "Yep. I totally get it. I feel that way, too, sometimes." And when my own inner voice is having a tantrum — usually a cacophony of self-loathing, self-victimization, and vicious self-criticism, I try to bring that compassion to myself, too. "I get it, Little Angry Sam Voice. I hear you. I see you."

### Being the Enlightened Witness

Emergency workers and trauma specialists tell us that the most helpful thing an untrained person can do for someone who is upset — anywhere from skinned-knee upset to just-emerged-from-a-bomb-site upset — is to be present with them. To sit calmly near them. To breathe. To validate. To maintain gentle eye contact, and to say, "I hear you. I see you." To be, as famed psychotherapist Alice Miller said, "an enlightened witness."

So if you've ever seen a grieving friend or an upset stranger, and you've hesitated to step in because you've thought, "I don't know what to say," it may help to know that you don't really need to say anything. You just need to be present, to validate, to stay calm, and to witness.

Of course, it is much easier to be an enlightened witness when the person who is upset is not upset with *us*. When people are upset with us, we want to defend ourselves. But as Byron Katie (one of my all-time most helpful personal-development teachers) says, "defense is the first act of war." In other words, when someone is attacking us, calling us names, criticizing us, picketing our front lawn — it can be hard to remember that one option we have is to say, "Yes. I hear you. What you say may be true."

This is a real brain-scrambler, until you remember that arguing with someone who is mad at you has never once helped resolve anything. It only leads to more yelling.

Can you imagine if, say, a group of anti-something protest-ers met a bunch of pro-something protesters, and instead of chanting and waving signs, they sat down, faced one another, and said, "Yes. I hear you. You feel like this is wrong. I can see how this idea is very upsetting to you. Tell me more about how you feel." Or, "Yes. I hear you. You feel like this is right. Tell me more about that."

## *Sometimes*

I think one of the loveliest words in the language is *sometimes*. It works great when you are accusing yourself or someone else of something. For example, if you're about to say or think, "You are so stupid!" you can perform a mental magic trick by adding the word *sometimes*.

So now the phrase is "You are so stupid sometimes."

And really, we all can agree with that. Yes. I am so stupid sometimes. And sometimes I am brilliant.

Try adding *sometimes* to any criticism, and watch it lose its teeth.

## All Feedback Is Love

My father was always a highly critical person. He always knew the right way to do something, and he would not hesitate to correct you should you be found not doing something his way. He had strong opinions about all things — even things he had absolutely no experience with. He was a classic mansplainer of the old school, and because he was tall, intelligent, and handsome and had the deep, resonant voice of a broadcaster, few ever questioned him or called him out. So he was able to live his life in a bubble in which he was always right and the rest of the world was, according to him, hopelessly wrong.

His highest possible praise was "Well, that's not too bad, is it?" This is what he said when my very first job in Hollywood was as a guest star on a hit sitcom, when my first book was published, when my sister gave him the most marvelous grandchildren on earth, and when my baby sister got sober.

After years of therapy and self-work, I was able to see that criticism was actually his love language. He genuinely thought he was helping by offering his unsought advice. Once I saw it that way, his harsh judgments actually became kind of sweet, instead of something that made me feel bad about myself. My sisters and I developed a running joke between us, that no matter what we did or said or bought or made for him, it was never going to be right.

Not long before my dad entered hospice care, he and I spent a fabulous afternoon together. At his request, I had bought us a huge lobster, and we ate the whole thing, with butter dripping down our chins. This was followed by his favorite dessert: a frozen Milky Way bar and a Coke. We joked around, told funny stories, and watched some TV together. He was being the best version of himself, jovial and charming — even when he found a way to criticize the way I cracked the lobster.

The next day I went to see him again, and he started out, again, in pretty good spirits. But then he started sniping at me. Criticizing my life choices, including my decision, 35 years prior, to drop out of Northwestern University to become an actor, which he said, "ruined my life." He made undeservedly mean comments about my ex-husbands. He threw around some casual cruelties about my sisters, too, and had some choice words about his neighbors, the government, and a few of his ex-wives.

"OK," I thought. "He's dying and he's frightened, and this is his way of staying in control." So I just nodded and said gently, "Well, yes…sometimes that's true."

Then he started in on my weight. He has criticized my body relentlessly my entire life.* He started going on and on about

---

*   Once, when I was still in high school, he offered me $50 for every five pounds I lost, which was (and is) a lot of money. At the time I was 5′ 11″ and 138 pounds, a perfectly healthy weight.

how heavy I was and how much it disturbed him to see me this way.

I could feel myself shrinking into myself, allowing myself to feel belittled and ashamed.

In a desperate grab for my own sanity, I started to pretend that I had an Intergalactic Language Translator (like on those futuristic space exploration shows, where the aliens can all magically understand one another) in the center of my forehead. And as he kept going on and on about how horrible I looked, I just kept thinking, "He's telling you he loves you. This is the only way he knows how to tell you he loves you. Be patient. He loves you."

I sat and watched him speak and continued to almost hypnotize myself with my mantra: "He loves you. He is saying, 'I love you.' Don't pay attention to his words. He loves you."

Finally, he wrapped up his tirade by saying, "Well…at least you aren't Walmart Fat."

And I said, "I love you, Daddy."

He was doing the best he could with the information he had, and so was I.

He was terrible and wonderful and terrible.

And he was ours.

## 15-Minute Experiment

Consider: Is there someone in your life who uses, or has used, criticism as a love language? Or maybe you do that? How can you translate or reinterpret those criticisms? Maybe "You're lazy" translates to "I worry that you don't have work that you love." Or perhaps "You're ugly" means "I find you so beautiful that I have to disguise my true feelings."

## What If...

What if every criticism you remember also represents a compliment you have forgotten, ignored, or dismissed?

## 23

# Overwhelm and Depression

Those of us who suffer from depression and anxiety often have overwhelm as one of our symptoms.

An unanswered phone call
Taxes — or really, any kind of official form
The thought of a difficult conversation
Contemplating our future
Being asked directions on a street corner

Any of these seemingly innocent and not-that-hard situations can cause the depressed mind to shut down entirely and want to crawl back into bed for all eternity.

Then well-intentioned people say, "Oh, you know, they say exercise is just as effective as antidepressants. Why don't you go for a run?"

Or try prayer.
Or a gluten-free diet.
Or getting more sleep.

Thanks, helpful people. You have just made my inner world — in which I am already convinced that everything is my fault — an even darker and more self-punitive place.

### Throwing Pebbles at Dinosaurs

As you know, depression is a blackhearted fuckshop of a disease — insidious and all-enveloping. Recently, after I'd been mostly symptom-free for the past year or so, the past few weeks have been a swirling nightmare. I was a bit shocked at how swiftly I fell and hit bottom.

Because I have "atypical depression" — which despite its name is actually quite common — I can function well in public situations. Atypical depression is not the "can't get out of bed and crying all day" kind of depression. It's the "inside a glass box" kind — it looks like everything's pretty normal, but on the inside you feel utterly alone and completely dissociated. It turns the whole world into a wavy-mirrored horror show. Distorted. Lonely. Grim.

I hung in there, though: fought it when I could fight, and lay down quietly when I could fight no more. I prayed, I walked, I did all the things people suggest you do when you're depressed (take a hike, do something nice for someone else, get a massage, make some art...), all of which are like throwing pebbles at a dinosaur.

Finally — yesterday — the cloud lifted, and so far I've had 24 hours of nonstop joy.

Here's what joy looks like: I can taste food. I can breathe. I can feel actual gratitude for my actual life. Nothing fancy. Just the amazing sensation of experiencing energy and desire and being able to think actual thoughts rather than just drown in a sea of self-loathing all day.

Normally I would keep this kind of thing quiet, because it's private, and in many ways, it's none of anyone's fucking business. But I realize that because of what I do and the books I write, people sometimes think that I never have a bad day. Which would be hilarious if the reality weren't so tragic.

So, to everyone who is forced to make the choice, every day, to stay on this grassy, ocean-y planet no matter how much it hurts: I salute you. I wish you forgiving friends, loving partners, and soft landings. I bless your beautiful sensitivity, your aching heart, and the spiritual mastery that you are demonstrating every time you don't just give the fuck up.

I won't presume to offer you advice. But I will remind you of this: the tragedy of depression is that it convinces you that you will never, ever, ever, ever, ever feel better. And that is a giant fucking lie. You will feel better. Maybe only one degree better, but still — better.

And you matter. You matter to me.

Thank you for listening. I love you.

## 15-Minute Experiment

I wrote "Throwing Pebbles at Dinosaurs" some years ago as a social media post, and I got an avalanche of response. Some from people who also have depression and were grateful to feel seen, and some from people who do not live with depression,[*] saying that this bit of writing helped them understand it better.

After it went semi-viral, I emailed a copy to some CEOs and business owners I know, with the reminder that, according to the World Health Organization, at least 5 percent of their workforce was, that very day, living with depression. I suggested that they may want to consider acknowledging and

---

[*] It's still a little bit amazing to me that some people — most, in fact — do not live with depression. Since I've had it my whole life, I can't really imagine what that's like. I also recently heard that many people do not have a voice in their head that narrates every dip dang moment of their entire lives. I'm agog.

going the extra mile to support those people and others who live with invisible diseases and disorders.

In my own business I have implemented a designated vocabulary so we can let each other know when we're not up to par, without having to go into all the details. For example, I might say, "I didn't finish writing that email copy. I'm a bit boneless these days." My team knows that means I am not feeling well and am taking extra time to rest. I am lucky because, as an entrepreneur, I can give myself and my team the freedom to move deadlines, change project parameters, and otherwise accommodate the vicissitudes of life without undue consequences. We regularly remind each other to drink more water, eat a real meal, get more sleep, or go for a walk, and, in fact, to prioritize those things over work tasks. I'd rather have a healthier employee long-term than a stressed-out one short-term, you know?

Now, I understand that you may not be in the fairly low-stakes business of personal development (I mean, what's the worst that happens if we screw up — an affirmation doesn't get written? Ha. Big deal.), but perhaps you can spend 15 minutes asking for advice from your team, family, or organization about how to best support each other emotionally and spiritually with clear-eyed compassion.

### What If...

What if your legacy is kindness?

# 24

# An Historical Perspective

I am constantly seeing articles citing how very much more stressful and overwhelming the world is now than it used to be. And everyone I know reflects on their growing-up years as "a simpler time." But was it, really?

## So Much Information Now

We hear the daily litany of world crises in the news, not to mention the minute-by-minute updates available on social media, and it just seems like there is way too much information flooding in each day.

There's a lot of news to keep track of. Once the news reporting stopped being one 30-minute TV program at 6 p.m. or an easily read daily newspaper, and the 24-hour news cycle began, the news became part of the entertainment industry. Rather than simply reporting noteworthy events, the media began to hype everything with breathless agony, because if it's an emergency, well, they know you are more likely to stay tuned. And the more you stay tuned, the more they can charge for advertising.

Now, news as specious entertainment is not new — it's as old as media itself — but cable news channels, podcasts, and on-line "reporting" have raised it to a new, and often distressingly anti-intellectual, art form.

## So Much Marketing and Advertising Now

And that's not even addressing the amount of marketing and advertising that comes at us from every corner.

Now consider this bit of gorgeous writing:

> It is true that the materialistic society, the so-called culture that has evolved under the tender mercies of capitalism, has produced what seems to be the ultimate limit of this worldliness. And nowhere, except perhaps in the analogous society of pagan Rome, has there ever been such a flowering of cheap and petty and disgusting lusts and vanities as in the world of capitalism, where there is no evil that is not fostered and encouraged for the sake of making money.
>
> We live in a society whose whole policy is to excite every nerve in the human body and keep it at the highest pitch of artificial tension, to strain every human desire to the limit and to create as many new desires and synthetic passions as possible, in order to cater to them with the products of our factories and printing presses and movie studios and all the rest.

Wow, right?

That was written by everyone's favorite Trappist monk, Thomas Merton, in his classic autobiography, *The Seven Storey Mountain*. And guess what? He wrote that in 1948.

So perhaps our feeling of being oppressed by the marketing of manufactured desire isn't a recent development, either.

## And Those Kids Today — They're Not Like We Were

You can find endless quotes from all of human history about "those kids today" not having any morals, not respecting their elders, and behaving lewdly. Some of these quotes seem a bit too perfect, like this one, often attributed to Socrates:

> The counts of the indictment are luxury, bad manners, contempt for authority, disrespect to elders, and a love for chatter in place of exercise....
>
> Children began to be the tyrants, not the slaves, of their households. They no longer rose from their seats when an elder entered the room; they contradicted their parents, chattered before company, gobbled up the dainties at table, and committed various offenses.

This quote is actually from Kenneth John Freeman, from his Cambridge dissertation on ancient Greece in 600 to 300 BCE, published in 1907. Freeman did not claim that it was a direct quote from Socrates or anyone else; instead, "he was presenting his own summary of the complaints directed against young people in ancient times."

Thus, we can safely conclude that older people have been telling younger people to get off their lawns for a few millennia now.

## Follow the Money

So — let us summarize:

News is always bad, and being fed an endless stream of it is no good for any of us. But they make a ton of money doing it, so it's not going to stop.

Marketing and advertising are competing for your attention and your money, and the way they get it is by convincing you that you are *just.not.good.enough.* unless you have what they are peddling. This makes them a ton of money, so they aren't going to stop, either.

The job of adolescents is to separate from their parents so they can go off and become independent adults, and the easiest way for them to do that is to pick something that will confuse and incense the older generation. They like to do this all together, so they can be different while being exactly like all their friends, who are also being different. The whole concept of adolescence has turned into an important marketing strategy that makes people a ton of money, so that's not going to stop, either.

## What to Do Next

**1) Do not look at the news first thing.** Spend your first hour or two in the morning doing healthful, soul-restoring activities. You know — like snuggling and taking the dog for a walk and talking with your kids while they are still in pajamas and stretching and kitchen dancing and spending 15 minutes on something that matters to you. Wait to check the news until later in the day. Believe me — if something big happens, you'll hear about it.

A ton of data shows that the way you spend the first hour of your day has an outsized effect on the rest of your day, so please don't start your morning by filling your brain with horrible stories of global atrocities. Let's wait until lunch for the atrocities, shall we?

**2) Unsubscribe from marketing emails.** Or at least create a separate email address or even just a folder to hold the promotional emails until you find it needful to see them. Block online ads when you can. Notice when you feel drawn to doing "recreational" shopping, and maybe experiment with some other activity instead. Look, I love to shop. Truly. But I notice that the slightly frenzied cart-filling that I do after midnight is not conducive to a peaceful mind or a joyful heart.

## But What about the State of the World???

I think we have allowed ourselves to become a bit confused about the natural behavior of humans in the world. Because we can *imagine* ourselves behaving better, we feel like we should be able to create that reality.

But it's not like we can look back and say, "Hey, remember when men and women really understood and respected one another and shared power and resources equally? Let's go back to doing that!"

Nope. Never happened. At least not in recorded history. Not even once, as far as I know.

Nor can we say, "Remember that time when all the races got along? Where we met people who were different from ourselves, and we all treated each other with compassion and curiosity?"

Yeah. Not so much. Seems like every tribe on earth has always referred to themselves as "The People" and everyone else as "The Barbarians." We are designed to like people who look like us and to mistrust everyone else. It's a survival thing.

"Remember when there was economic parity in the world?"
"Remember when no one used starvation as a way to control large numbers of people?"
"Remember when there was no such thing as corruption?"
"Remember when creepy old dudes didn't consider younger people sexual prey?"

Nope.
Nope.
Nope.
Nope.

I find this long view of our history of behaving badly oddly comforting. Of course I want to see it changed, and I do my part every chance I get. But understanding that just because I can conceive of a world in which practical wisdom, proper self-management, justice, and bravery are our governing principles does not mean that I can make it so. Or perhaps even that it should be so.

More important are the other things that are, and have always been, true of us. All people, throughout all time:

We want to love and be loved.
We want for our work to matter.
We want our children to succeed and be happy.
We want to eat good food and laugh at good jokes.
We grieve.
We are humbled.
We find delight in the smallest of details.

And we never stop working for a better tomorrow. Even if it's just for 15 minutes a day.

## 15-Minute Experiment

Forget about global injustice for a moment. What can you do for 15 minutes that will adjust the injustice in your own home? Can you address the equitable division of labor? The equitable sharing of the remote control? Can you take a stand against thoughtless sexism, racism, or other *isms*? What if you made an effort to find the *good* news in the world?

## What If...

What if you remember that you are not in control of anything other than yourself?

# 25

# Intermezzo: All This Wanting Is Killing You

Stop wanting.
Quit it.
Quiet down.
This grasping — this ache — this picking apart — this
    chronic dissatisfaction
is murdering you.
Your desire for everything to be different —
Your body
Your lover
Your bank account
Your mom.

Shhhhhh.

Be content with all that is in you right now.

You already have everything.
You already have everything.
You already have everything.

(Has your ego stopped arguing with me yet?)

You want love.
You are love.

You want to be understood.
Relax in the light that limns your every corner and crevice.

You want to be different.
No, you don't.

You want everyone else to be different so you can get more
    approval.

Even though you know that more approval from others
    doesn't really help.

What does help
is your approval of you.

Your approval of your life.

Your kind and benevolent eye
Forgiving your trespasses,
Appreciating your daily bread,
Laughing at your own jokes.

You have been craving you all along.

All you want for Christmas — is you.

# 26

# The 15-Minute Method at Work

I have never had a job in corporate America.* The world of cubicles and multi-tier management structures is completely foreign to me. As a broke actor in Chicago and then LA, with a million part-time jobs and then working for myself as a writer, teacher, and entrepreneur, I've never had a steady paycheck. I drive past those big industrial parks and office buildings, and I wonder what people do in there. I sometimes joke that I feel like I can hear them crying. People in the know assure me that, indeed, many are crying. In the washrooms, at their desks, or just silently inside. Some from boredom, some from frustration, and some because of the freedom they crave.

I suspect that if they were given 15 minutes a day to work on something that mattered to them, they might feel a bit better.

I have a dream that everywhere — in organizations both big and small — spending the first 15 minutes of your workday engaged in a project that is meaningful to you becomes standard

---

\* I have been a whitewater river guide. I have done scarf-tying demonstrations in department stores. I've taught improv. I've produced radio dramas. I've sold ballet tickets via telemarketing. I've performed murder mystery dinner theater. I've cocktailed and worked retail and had temp gigs of every stripe. I even once got paid to fly back and forth from Burbank to San Francisco a bunch of times because a rich guy was trying to game the airlines' mileage points system. But somehow, corporate America and I never got together.

practice. And I'm not the only one who thinks so. Google famously instituted the "20% Project," which allowed employees to spend up to one full day a week working on projects of their choice — whether or not the project was directly related to their job title. Other companies, such as the BBC, Apple, and 3M, have also implemented versions of this idea. With varying success, it must be said, but still — it seems worth further experimentation, don't you think?

I also have a hunch that if employees were encouraged to *talk* about their 15-minute activities, they might grow to appreciate each other in new ways. Can you imagine the chitchat?

"What are you spending your 15 minutes on today?"

"Oh, I'm creating a new recipe that's kind of like a paella, so I was researching where to source saffron. You?"

"I wrote some crappy poetry."

"I LOVE crappy poetry! I wrote some crappy poetry last week! Let's have a coffee!"

How many times have you met someone and felt sort of neutral about them, but then you found out that you both love fly-tying or Zen archery, and the next thing you knew, you were besties? Right? See where I'm going with this?

Take Chris, who works down the hall, whom you think is an imperious know-it-all with a bad attitude. But then you find out that Chris was an Olympic-level equestrian — well, suddenly Chris's superior tone makes a lot more sense. Chris is a person on a lifelong quest for excellence. Plus, maybe Chris has some good advice about your preteen daughter's choice of riding camp.

When you know what people love to do in their spare time, you can connect with them on a whole other level. You can appreciate the fullness of their personalities and the scope of their wisdom. You can learn from them, share with them, and even encourage them to bring their additional skills to the workplace.

I remember reading a study that showed an easy way to improve meetings: Ask each participant to introduce themselves and include two or three details about themselves that are apart from work. Maybe something about their hometown or their cultural background and a topic they wish they had time to study more closely. Or whatever. The idea being that if you take a moment to remind people of their whole selves and the diversity of their experience before, say, a brainstorming meeting, they will participate more and have better ideas.

This simple introductory process gets everyone's voice into the room right away. Which means they'll be more likely to speak up later. I know this from my improv comedy background: If you want the audience to shout out suggestions at any point in the show, you have to ask them to do it for the first time right at the beginning. If you have people sit in silence for twenty minutes and then ask them for a suggestion, you won't get it, because you've trained them to sit in silence. Thus, if you want people talking in your meetings, you need to get them talking right away, and preferably about something they are actually interested in. Like, say, themselves.

So letting Kai introduce themself as not just, "Hi, I'm Kai from Sales," but rather, "Hi, I'm Kai from Sales. I was born in Belize, and lately I've been really enjoying baking vegan desserts," means that Kai won't just contribute from a "Sales" perspective but will feel free to braid in their other life experiences, thus leading to better, more original ideas and outcomes.

If you are a business owner, or you run a team or a department, or you convene groups of any kind (book groups, worship teams, running clubs…), I encourage you to implement this daily 15-minute experiment for a month: Choose a 15-minute window that will work for you and your people. I recommend mornings because by afternoon, the day tends to get away from a person. Tell everyone that for this month, every day from 9 to 9:15 a.m., or whatever time you've chosen, is "experimentation" time, and they should work, uninterrupted, on something that matters to them. This might be related to their job, but not necessarily. Maybe it's taking a quick walk around the block to get some air or sitting quietly in prayer or meditation. Maybe it's writing a book or a blog post, or building skills, or coding something cool, or anything that would make a positive difference for themselves or for the group and would otherwise not get done. This is *not* a time to catch up on emails or their personal to-do lists or even their work to-do lists. This is a time to nourish themselves.

I bet you will see engagement go up. You've heard about how 77 percent of employees are disengaged, right? 15 minutes of freedom to play seems to me like a cost-free solution to an otherwise very expensive problem.

Unless I'm wrong. Which would be equally interesting to me. So please try it, and then reach out to me at Sam@TheReal SamBennett.com, OK?

Together, we can reduce the snuffling sound of corporate crying! YAY!

## 15-Minute Experiment

Spend 15 minutes writing down all the reasons this would be a great idea for your group, team, or friend group, and then also log all the reasons it would never work. Then take both lists and go talk to your boss, team, or group about this idea and see what happens. Remind everyone that it's an experiment. I double-dog dare you.

## What If...

What if 15 minutes a day is the lever you need to move the world?

# 27

# Clutter Scoring

The way the magazines talk about it, you'd think clutter was the worst thing that could ever happen to a person. But it seems to me that clutter, like most things, exists on a spectrum and is subject to personal preference.

Rather than holding ourselves to some perfecty-schmerfecty ideal in which the counters are always clear and the clothes are always neatly put away, perhaps we could create our own matrix.

Here's my Clutter Clearing for Grown-Ups quiz:

1. If you are looking for something, does it usually take you more than 10 minutes to find it?
2. In the past year, have you spent more than you would have liked replacing things that got broken because they weren't properly stored?
3. In the past year, have you spent more than you would have liked buying duplicates of things you already had but couldn't find?
4. Do you have a lot of things with the price tags still on them or still in the original packaging, unused?
5. Do you have a lot of things that you don't use but are keeping "just in case"?
6. Do you have a lot of things that you would not necessarily have picked out for yourself, but because they used to belong to other people, you feel obligated to keep them?

7. Do you have a lot of half-finished projects around the house?
8. Do you have a junk drawer?
9. Do you have a junk room, junk closet, junk garage, or junk storage unit?
10. Do you feel like the clutter, dust, dander, dirt, and excess stuff in your house are affecting your mental and/or physical health?

You can give yourself a moment to consider every "yes" answer, and see how you feel. Because that's the only part that matters. Me giving you some random scoring system ("More than 5 points? You're a Plenty Biggo Messy Bunny for sure!" #ugh) is dismissive and, frankly, irrelevant.

I think if the way you live is joyful and life-expanding, then you're fine. Keep what you want to keep; it's nobody's business but your own.

On the other hand, if you feel like your stuff is costing you time, peace of mind, money you don't have, and/or peaceful relationships with partners, neighbors, or family, you may want to look at that, even if it's only one shelf or drawer that's bothering you.

You may have only one "yes" answer — maybe it's the stuff you have inherited from others, in which case you might want to do some inner work on grief, forgiveness, family systems, and identity. As the eldest, I have often kept things because I felt like I had to be the family historian or the holder of memories — keeping things for posterity. Turns out I'm allowed to keep only the stuff that's meaningful to me. Other people don't actually need me to be the librarian of their past.

I will use my Big Teacher Voice when it comes to question 10, though. If you feel that the amount, organization, cleanliness, and/or low quality of stuff in your house is having an adverse effect on your health, then I must insist that you take action. If others in your life are expressing concern, take that seriously. And if you can't have people over because you are embarrassed to have them see your life, that, too, is an important sign that you are ready to change.

Life is much too short and precious to be sacrificed for a bunch of stuff. I strongly advise finding yourself some loving, cheerful professional help. There are lots of organizers who can work in-person or remotely, many who will work for free, and they can offer you the support and systems you need to make your home healthy for you and those you love.

I guess I feel about clutter the same way I do about weight: mostly, I couldn't care less, unless it starts affecting the quality of your life — then I want to advocate for your well-being.

I refuse to demonize clutter. I don't think it's a moral issue, though with the amount of pressure I see people put on themselves, you'd think that the cleanliness/godliness connection was a real thing.

I sell a mug on my website that says, "Art Before Housework" and another version that says "Poetry Before Housework." No one cares if you do those dishes now or later today. But the 15 minutes you spend on work that matters to you could impact generations to come.

## 90-Second Doodle on Clutter

Take 90 seconds to draw out how your clutter makes you feel. Use stick figures, shapes, and scrawl. This is not art — it's a self-improvement doodle so you can get a visual on how you're feeling. Don't think. Just make a picture of how it feels. Keep drawing until 90 seconds are up.

Now, observe the doodle. What do you notice? How would you title it? What feelings does it bring up for you? If it feels enriching to do so, consider journaling or writing some poetry or keeping going with the drawing thing. Anything to get those feelings out of wherever they've been hiding (in your closet behind that old bridesmaid dress?) and out into the open sunshine.

Next step: Grab another page of doodle paper and draw what it would feel like if your house were perfectly organized for your tastes. Or think of it this way: If you had a magic wand and could make anything happen, what would you like your house, desk, closet, etc., to look like? You don't have to draw the house itself — just the feeling it would give you. Again, draw for 90 seconds without editing.

What does this new doodle have to say to you? What clues are there for you?

## Other People's Clutter

If there are other people involved in your clutter situation — and isn't other people's clutter *so* much more annoying than your own? — you may want to do this exercise with them, so you can all have a conversation that is not so much about this item or that, but rather about how it all feels to each of you, and what you want.

Once you know what you want, you can make a 15-minutes-a-day plan to get there.

I love the story of my client and friend Julie who moved cross-country into her mother's house to care for her mom during the last year or so of her mom's life, then inherited the house. Feeling completely overwhelmed by the lifetime of stuff her mom had accumulated, while simultaneously working through her own grief, Julie started with her mom's papers, of which there were piles and piles.

Every day, for 15 minutes, she would go to her mom's desk and sort and file papers, finding lots of trash and a few treasures along the way. She realized that her mom's record player was in the same room, so Julie started playing the old albums as she sorted, tossed, and filed. Then she found a box of lovely old stationery, so she decided to start sending notes and letters to friends, family, and loved ones. This meant, of course, that she had to walk down to the mailbox each day, which got her out into the fresh air, and occasionally meeting her new neighbors along the way.

This is how one 15-minute practice spawned another, which gave way to another, which created one more. Now Julie has a wonderful daily routine in which she attends to her own paperwork, enjoys music, writes, and takes a walk, and the whole thing takes maybe an hour in total.

Last I heard, Julie had completed her mom's desk and had moved on to clearing an old linen closet and turning it into an arts-and-crafts supply closet.

All in just 15 minutes a day.

## 15-Minute Experiment

Set your timer and spend 15 minutes clearing out some space that's been bugging you. If it's a small area, you might be able to complete it, but otherwise it's fine to clear just part of a shelf or drawer. Notice how even a small improvement makes a difference.

## *What If...*

What if you knew someone was just waiting for the opportunity to help you?

## 28

# How to Say No without Punishment

Someone has asked you to do something you don't want to do.

Here are some responses you might want to practice in advance, so you're never in a position of saying yes when what you really mean is no. Adjust to fit your own voice, obvs.

"No, thank you."

"Thanks for thinking of me. I'm going to need to get back to you on that."

"That's a bit outside my sphere at the moment. But thanks for thinking of me."

"I'm not able to make time for that right now."

"I can't give that the energy or attention it deserves, and I don't want to let you down, so I'm going to say no for now."

"That's not possible for me now, but please ask me again next time."

"That's not going to work for me."

"I love your enthusiasm, but I don't share it. I don't think I'm the right person for this."

"That is so interesting. It's not for me, though."

"I'd be happy to serve as a sounding board as you move forward, but that's about all I can offer."

"Nope. That sounds awful."

"Remember when you asked me to be honest with you? OK — I'm not interested."

"I'm having a values conflict with this."

"That's not for me."

"I'm afraid that will interfere with my quest for world
      domination. Thanks, though."

"You're so cute."

"Oh dear God — no."

"Aw hell no."

"Hard pass."

"This doesn't feel like a good fit for me."

"I would, but I promised myself after last time: never
      again."

"Can we talk about this tomorrow?"

"I don't care for that. No, thank you."

"I've promised my family that I won't add any addi-
      tional projects to my calendar until after XYZ, so
      I'm just not available."

"Keep walking, sister!"

"This is a bit outside my purview."*

## 15-Minute Experiment

Read the list above out loud, with feeling. Add a few of your
own. See if you can find a way to offer one good, solid *No* today.

### What If...

What if you finally said yes in a way that really mattered?
What if you finally said no in a way that really mattered?

---

\*     Use words like *purview* often enough, and people might stop talking to you
completely.

# 29

# Why This 15-Minute Thing Actually Works

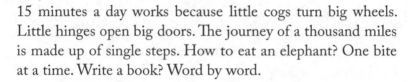

15 minutes a day works because little cogs turn big wheels. Little hinges open big doors. The journey of a thousand miles is made up of single steps. How to eat an elephant? One bite at a time. Write a book? Word by word.

We all want a whole weekend to clear out the garage. But somehow, that weekend never comes. Some of us would like three months at a villa in Provence to finish our novel, and somehow that's not showing up, either.

And you may have promised yourself that come summer, or come retirement, you are finally going to get to all those hobbies and activities you love. Yet even when that time comes, you find yourself not doing any of them at all.

Putting off big projects for a mythical "someday" is, in its own way, understandable. Particularly when the big projects are hard or have the potential of changing your life. As much as we may dream about changing our lives, most of us never do. As much as we crave novelty, our desire for predictability usually wins out.

Little tasks get postponed, too, don't they? Minor annoyances don't get fixed. That pile in the corner on the exercise bike just...stays there.

We call this procrastination. But *procrastination* is another one of those words that has come to mean too many things. You say,

"I'm procrastinating," when perhaps what you really mean is:

I'm afraid of this task.
I'm afraid of the consequences of doing this task.
I'm afraid of judgment.
I'm bored stiff by the very idea of doing this task.
I feel this task is beneath me.
This task feels messy to me.
I'm hoping if I ignore it long enough, it will go away.
I am waiting for a perfect moment.
An element of divine timing hasn't kicked in yet.
I resent this task.
I'm too old for this shit.
Someone else should do this.
I'm missing some information, and I don't feel like finding out what I need to know.
I have a childish fear about this.
I have a full-on phobia about this.
I think if I do this now, it will mean more work for me down the road.

## 15-Minute Experiment

Read the above list out loud and see if any resonate as you say them. "Can't I just read it silently to myself?" Sure. But then you won't have the opportunity to surprise yourself. Maybe add in some new phrases of your own. Then spend whatever's left of your 15 minutes writing (dancing, singing, rapping, drawing…) about what hit home for you and what's behind it.

## What If…

What if there isn't a right way, there's just *your* way?

# 30

# I Lost It at the Diner

Anyone who knows me will tell you: I almost never lose my temper.

I consider my ability to stay calm in stressful, high-pressure, and argumentative circumstances to be one of my superpowers.

But the other day I LOST IT.

At a diner.

About breakfast.

See, I was out early running errands, and it suddenly occurred to me that I could try out this nearby diner for the first time and treat myself to a nice breakfast.

I *love* diner food.

When I get there and the server points out a booth to me, I scooch myself in. I am very pleased that the decor is classic — refreshingly unironic — and the food smells great.

Especially the biscuits and gravy, which I consider a rare treat indeed.

I decide to order something with the unappetizing name of "The Kitchen Sink," which is all the bits and pieces of all the things I want to try. This is excellent because I *love* a sample platter. So a diner-breakfast sample platter is kind of my ideal order.

Except the way the dish is described on the menu, they pile up all the elements in a stack on one plate. Home fries on the bottom, then eggs, then a biscuit and gravy on that, then bacon. I think this sounds sort of gross.

So when the server comes to take my order, I explain that I would like The Kitchen Sink, but may I please have it spread out instead of stacked up? Or even on different plates?

"No."

Huh?

"We don't serve it that way."

OK…um…why???

"Let me get the manager."

Wow. That escalated quickly. I'm puzzled, but not mad.

Now the manager comes over, a short, thick-necked man who has a bulldog-like demeanor.

"Is there a problem?" he gruffs.

I explain about wanting a deconstructed Kitchen Sink.

"No."

HUH? "Why?"

"We were getting slammed with substitutions, and…"

Oh! I get it! Yes! I've worked in hospitality and food service, and I get it — substitutions are a nightmare. I totally get it. I clarify that I'm happy to accept the meal as cooked, I just want it spread out a bit.

"No."

Wow. I ask again, "Why?"

"These are the rules," says Mr. Bulldog. "The government has rules. I have rules. We all have to follow the rules."

The government has rules about my breakfast?

"Can I get you something else?"

Now this would be my big opportunity to smile sweetly and order everything in that Kitchen Sink thing, but à la carte. Or pick something else on the menu to eat. Or simply ask for a hot tea and take some time to consider the life choices that brought me here.

But I don't.

Because, of all the things that piss me off (and again — there aren't that many of those things), the phrase "That's just the rules, ma'am" is the worst.

I am incensed, and the next thing I know, I am in my car, pulling away, still hungry, and now angry and crying.

To be fair, I've been doing a lot of crying the past few weeks, so even in this moment, I know that the tears may not be about the diner.

I try to calm down. I remember I still haven't eaten, which is probably why I'm reacting so strongly. "Eat something," I think. I pull into good old reliable Starbucks and order a tea and a breakfast egg-and-sausage sandwich.*

---

* Which is an all-piled-up thing, I know. #icontradictmyself #icontainmultitudes

135

While I'm waiting for my order, I make a point to notice the other people in Starbucks being human with one another. There are two teenage girls bent over a phone. There is a couple having an intense discussion about something that happened yesterday. There are two workers outside, stringing up holiday lights.

Usually, noticing other people just being their dear human selves is enough to cheer me up and calm me down. Not today, though.

I get back in my car and do some of my favorite 4-7-8 breathing (inhale for 4, hold for 7, exhale for 8) which almost always calms me down like magic. Not today.

I consider calling a friend to vent. Then I remember how my friend Billy always referred to that "venting" as "praying the problem."

In other words, any time you find yourself repeating a story over and over — especially one in which you are the innocent victim — you are energizing that story. You are keeping yourself hooked into a certain version of reality. So while normally I would be perfectly happy to dump this whole silly story on a friend so that I can be told how right I am and how dumb everyone else is, I choose not to. So — no venting. Not today.

As I drive home from Starbucks, I catch myself rerunning the conversation with Mr. Bulldog Manager in my head, especially the part at the end, where I just wiggled out of the booth, grabbed my bag, and left without saying much. I keep mentally rewriting better and better lines of dialogue for myself.

You may have noticed in your own life that replaying old conversations, or rehearsing conversations you haven't had yet, is not the highest and best use of your imagination. I know that replaying the incident over and over is not going to help me, no matter how clever my esprit de l'escalier.* So I stop with the reruns.

OK, time for the big medicine. I start to run through Byron Katie's Four Questions. In case you aren't familiar with Katie's work (TheWork.com), I cannot recommend it highly enough. I find her simple process to be revelatory, every single time.

But not today.

ARRRGHHHHH.

I am almost home. I have run through my favorite tools for self-management, and I am still mad.

I resolve that this diner dude and his dumb breakfast rules are *not* going to ruin my day. No, sir! Not today, sir!

So I call the restaurant and ask to speak to the manager. I introduce myself, and then I say that I am calling to apologize to him. I explain that it was unlike me to storm out like that, and I am sorry for behaving that way.

"I just want people to have a nice breakfast," he blusters, still defensive.

I say I understand, and I thank him for hearing me out. As he is hanging up, he sort of mumbles something I can't hear. I hope it was something nice.

He doesn't apologize.

---

\* Literally: the wit, or inspiration, of the staircase. Leave it to the French to come up with a term that describes the thing you think of to say when you've already stormed out, slammed the door, and made it halfway down the stairwell. Genius.

He certainly doesn't say he hopes they'll see me again soon. He isn't even particularly nice about me apologizing.

But I wasn't calling him because I wanted him to apologize.

I wasn't calling him to try to make him feel bad about his behavior.

I was calling because I felt bad about *my* behavior.

I wasn't apologizing to him because he "deserved" it. I was apologizing to him because *I* deserved it.

And I felt so much better afterward.

There were a million different ways I could have handled this diner situation. Obviously, it was a completely minor matter to which I had an outsized emotional response.

That's what happens when your values get stepped on.

So when you find yourself getting unusually peeved about something or someone, ask yourself, "Which values of mine are getting squashed here? And how can I realign myself with my values right now?"

I called him because kindness and good humor and empathy and finding creative solutions are some of my most important values, and when Mr. Bulldog demonstrated none of those, I freaked out.

The fact that I was able to unfreak myself out in less than an hour is the result of thousands of hours of spiritual study and personal development.

I used my tools:

1. Eat something. Drink something reassuring.

2. Notice all the humans around you being so very human.
3. Try 4-7-8 breathing.
4. Avoid "praying the problem." Quit collecting evidence about how right you are.
5. Stay in the present moment. Do not allow your imagination to get stuck replaying, rewriting, or rehearsing hard conversations.
6. Explore TheWork.com by Byron Katie.
7. Examine your values, and notice which ones are at play.
8. Treat others as you would like to be treated. Especially if they don't deserve it.

## 15-Minute Experiment

Make a list of some of the tools that work for you when you get upset. For bonus points, add a second list of things that history has taught you do *not* work for you when you get upset.

## What If...

What if every single person on earth is here to be your spiritual teacher? (And if so, what are they teaching you today?)

# 31

# Double or Halve

Having trouble keeping going? Or even just getting started? Try doubling or halving your goal. Here are some thoughts to play with.

### Where are you underestimating yourself?

When I was learning weightlifting, my coach taught me that most people will underestimate how much weight they can lift, or how many reps they can do, by half. So if they say they can lift 75 pounds, they can probably lift 150, and if they say they can do 10 reps, they can probably do 20.

What if you can do double what you think you can do?

### Where are you taking more time than you need?

When you say, "I need some time to think about it," how much time do you actually need? Could you challenge yourself to make some decisions more quickly? Sales training has taught me that many people will double the amount of time that they say they need to make a decision. So if someone says they need four days to think about it, offer them two days and see what happens.

What if you gave up dithering, pondering, and second-guessing?

*Where could you cut something by half and still be satisfied?*

I notice that restaurant portions are twice as big as I want them to be, so I now automatically only eat half and then bring the rest home. Luckily, I adore leftovers.

What if you only need half of what you think you need?

*What could you axe without really noticing?*

The Pareto principle (the 80/20 rule) tells us that we use 20 percent of our stuff 80 percent of the time, and that 20 percent of your clients are bringing in 80 percent of your revenue. So, following this principle, you could easily get rid of half of your possessions and half of your lowest-paying clients without really noticing.

What could you lose without even missing it?

*Where could slowing down bring you better results?*

Caress or pet the person or animal you love at half speed and watch them melt. Halve your speed again and watch them swoon.

Where could taking more time get you more of what you want?

## 15-Minute Experiment

Make a short list of three to five things you could double, halve, or axe, and experiment with one today.

## What If...

What if you took the easy way out? (Think: shortcuts, graceful exits, elegant solutions, cutting to the chase, and doing the simplest possible thing with no embellishment.)

# 32

# Grumpy Magic

How can you create magical results when you feel utterly de-moralized?

Can you be in a place to receive a miracle when you are feeling burnt-out and put-upon?

Does hopelessness contain the key to joy?

As much as I am a fan of positive thinking and positive mental attitudes and being positively positive about all the positives, I notice that pessimists still manage to get rich and fall in love, and mean-spirited people can achieve great things.

And perhaps there's something about all this oppressive optimism and relentless "love and light" peddling that is actually keeping you from getting what you want.

Let's talk about counterintuitive ways to create a magical life when you're feeling grumpy, grody, and mad, shall we?

## Three Steps to Grumpy Magic

When you feel exhausted, disconnected, unwell, and like you've lost your mojo, it's easy to slip into feeling powerless. Follow along on this self-evaluation with me, and let's see if you can remember your power and make a bit of a shift.

### Step 1: Handle Your Immediate Needs

Anytime things feel off, it's worth doing the HALTT-G test. This is a slightly expanded version of the self-care practice known by the common acronym HALT. It stands for "hungry, angry, lonely, tired," and the idea is that when you are feeling low, you stop and ask yourself if the cause might be one of those states, which you can then take steps to remedy. I've added in a T for *thirsty* and a G for *grieving*.

So if you are feeling crappy in mood or in body, first check to see if you are in need of some physical or emotional sustenance.

**Hungry:** When I get upset, the last thing I want to do is eat. And then, of course, my blood sugar tanks and I feel worse. So please eat at least a little bit of something. Bonus points if you can actually taste it and enjoy it.

**Angry:** You may have dissociated yourself from the word *angry*. Many women and Midwesterners refuse to ever consider themselves as angry.* So you may find yourself using words like *frustrated, annoyed, in a bad mood, irritated*, or *disappointed* instead. Let me invite you to own your anger. Try saying it out loud to yourself: "I am absolutely furious." Feels kinda good, huh?

Anger is a sign that your values are being stomped on, your vision is being ignored, or you are feeling disregarded, disrespected, physically or emotionally hurt, or not in control. These are important signals for you to recognize, and while I know you can internalize it all, or redirect it (yelling in traffic, for example, instead of yelling at your boneheaded boss), I might suggest you experiment with more productive ways to express the full force of your feelings without being disrespectful or cruel.

When I need to express anger, I like to call it "bringing the hammer of sunshine down upon them." I suggest reading up on "nonviolent communication" as pioneered by Marshall B.

---

* I'm kidding — this problem knows no gender or geography.

Rosenberg, PhD, to find out how to express strong feelings without violence. It's life-changing stuff.

There is also such a thing as "agitated depression," in which crankiness and anxiety are symptoms of a depressive disorder. You may want to look into that one, too.

**Lonely:** You may have heard about the epidemic of loneliness in the world, and the devastating health consequences thereof. Everyone needs to feel seen and heard. Everyone needs to feel that they belong.

We are tribal animals — meant to live in a group — and abandonment is one of our worst fears. And while of course I want you to be surrounded by people who love and respect you and laugh at all your jokes all the time, I realize that's not always possible, so I'm going to suggest something a little unusual: find yourself an imaginary friend. I once conquered my loneliness and anxiety about driving across a very scary, tall suspension bridge by imagining that Lyle Lovett was in the back seat, talking me through it.* I've confided terrible fears to my cats. I've confessed to a hotel room pillow, and I've prayed to a full moon.

The answer to loneliness is communion, and luckily, you can do that by yourself if necessary.

**Tired:** Sleep deprivation has been known as an effective form of torture for centuries, because it has the power to ruin you. Fatigue is more than a minor complaint — it will throw off your entire system. According to the CDC, one in three adults reports not getting enough sleep, and that leads to impaired judgment, poor mood, and all manner of negative health

---

\* Pick your own comforting imaginary friend, of course. I wouldn't expect everyone to find the mythical presence of Mr. Lovett as calming as I do.

consequences. Pay attention to your sleep hygiene, and if you have chronic sleep difficulties, please see a medical professional.

**Thirsty:** My mother always said that by the time you feel thirsty you are already dehydrated, so you should drink before you think you need it. Wise woman, my mom. It's been reported that 75 percent of Americans are chronically dehydrated, either because they don't drink enough fluids to begin with or they mitigate the positive effects with too much caffeine and salt. You can improve your mental processing by increasing your intake of water, and I can't think of a much easier way to make your life better.

**Grieving:** I don't know if science has noticed this, but I'm pretty sure that grieving makes you clumsy. It can also make you absent-minded, short-tempered, sleepy, dopey, bashful, possibly sneezy, and definitely grumpy. There is no appropriate advice for grieving because there is no appropriate way to do it. You cannot grieve correctly, nor incorrectly. There is no set duration. Grief comes in waves — sometimes the small, lapping waves of a duck pond at sunset, and sometimes a ferocious tsunami. Experience your grief however it comes, and remember to grant yourself extra grace during the more intense moments, OK?

### Step 2: Figure Out Where You Are on the Continuum

Let's forget about what you want for a sec. Let's deal with where you are. Let's be specific.

First, write out or say a statement about how you are feeling right now. Now, please score that statement on an intensity scale of 1 to 5 (1 being mildly irritated, 5 being the extreme).

Next, please name and fill in the phrases that — for you — make up the surrounding numbers. This is an entirely subjective exercise designed to give you a sense of where you are emotionally and where you might go. So if I write, "I'm pissed off at my partner" and give that a 3, then I might fill in 1 through 5 like this:

1 = It's cute when my partner is such a brat.
2 = I'm going to have to ask them to knock that shit off again.
3 = I'm pissed off at my partner.
4 = I'm starting to tally up my list of grievances, and I'm working up a big head of steam.
5 = Prepare for the Wrath of Kali.

Here's another example: let's say I want to take today off work because I'm not feeling strong or healthy in my body, and I'm at a 3 because it's been going on for a while, I might fill in the spectrum like this:

1 = Meh. I'm OK.
2 = I need to get some more rest.
3 = I need to take today off work.
4 = I've been resting and taking time off, and I still feel like total crapola.
5 = Time to call in the medical professionals.

Filling in the rest of the spectrum is important, because sometimes you are not very precise in your language, as in:

1 = I'm fine.
2 = Oh, I'm fine.
3 = Fine. Everything's fine.
4 = I'M FINE.
5 = Total hysterical breakdown.

And some of you have a really high tolerance for pain, so your version of "ow" is someone else's version of "call an ambulance."

Take a moment right now to get clear about what your current feeling continuum is.

At what point do you want to take action? How about now? What action might at least move you down a notch? Try to figure out what that is, and then do it.

### Step 3: Mine Your Grumpiness for Clues

Here's how to transform your grumpiness into a unique plan for success. This step requires some brief visualization/imagination work, which I know some people find annoying, but trust me — it's only for a moment.

1. Think about the thing you want. The thing you wish would magically appear. The thing whose absence is making you grumpy.
2. Now think about the benefit you seek — what would having that thing give you?
3. Consider where or when in your life you already have that benefit.
4. Picture yourself in that setting, and let yourself enjoy the feeling of it. Flood your mind with gratitude for the benefit.
5. Now see what your clever self comes up with when you consider the situation from a place of "already having" instead of "needing."

Let's try an example:

1. I'm thinking, "I want more money." I wish money would magically appear. The absence of money is making me grumpy.
2. The benefit of having more money would be feeling *relaxed and expansive.*

3. Where in my life do I already feel *relaxed and expansive*? Answer: under my fluffy down comforter!
4. I flood my mind with gratitude for my comforter. I imagine myself under my comforter feeling *relaxed and expansive*. I realize I don't need money to have the feeling I crave. That's relaxing to know. (But I still want more money.)
5. Now I ask my clever self: What happens when I consider the situation of "wanting to have more money" from the perspective of already feeling relaxed and expansive? Where can my fluffy comforter guide me?

Maybe I could write a new business plan in bed.

Or I could consider ways to make money while I sleep. Passive income, anyone?

I could look for new clients who share a relaxed and expansive worldview.

I could start a blog, podcast, or video series called "Pillow Talk" and interview other people (who are also in bed) about their financial philosophy and how it relates to their bedding, and become a massive viral sensation.*

## 15-Minute Experiment

Use your imagination and your ability to make unusual connections to both calm yourself down and think of some fun, or grumpy, 15-minute activities to do.

## *What If...*

What if you loosened up a bit and allowed some mystery, some magic, and even some silliness to guide you?

---

\* Hey, weirder things have happened.

# 33
# Talent Is Irrelevant

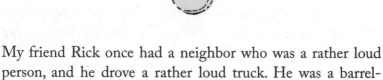

My friend Rick once had a neighbor who was a rather loud person, and he drove a rather loud truck. He was a barrel-chested guy with a cheerful disposition. He was always happy to help out any of the neighbors when they needed to move something heavy, and he would often take it upon himself to mow the yard of the older folks who lived across the street. He was always available if anyone wanted a pal to sit on the porch, drink a beer, and shoot the shit with. In short, he was a great neighbor. Let's say his name was Doug.

When Doug would get a few beers in him, he sometimes would imitate being an opera singer. He thought it was hilarious. But Doug actually had a really beautiful voice. His "fake" opera singing was quite glorious. When Rick said, "Hey, Doug — you have a real talent there. Maybe you should take a voice lesson or join a choir or something," Doug just laughed it off. He could no more imagine himself a serious singer than the man in the moon.

Doug had a natural talent — but it didn't mean anything to him.

Maybe you have a talent like that, too? Something you've always been naturally good at but dismissed as meaningless or inconsequential? Perhaps you can whip up a gourmet meal out of whatever's left in the fridge. Or maybe you can draw cartoons.

I knew a theater producer who was amazing at rhymes. For opening night of our show, she wrote us all an elaborate rhyming poem featuring our names, our characters' names, and some tidbit about each of us. It was kind of epic, but she laughed it off as a party trick.

Now, I'm not saying that you should immediately run out and monetize your talent. But you might want to lean into it a bit more, yes?

One of the things you learn working in show business is that talent is fairly meaningless. Lots of untalented people succeed, and some people with unbelievable talent get ignored. I suspect it's partly why Hollywood can be so weird — everyone who succeeds there is acutely aware that there are 10 other people who are just as good as they are, and who could take their place any second if needed. It all feels very "luck of the draw."

So if talent doesn't matter, what does matter? If you're holding yourself back because you think you're not talented enough to try, perhaps you could remember that the following habits will make you welcome wherever you may go.

- **Showing up.** Preferably 15 minutes early, and never, ever, ever late.
- **Being prepared.** Do your research, study the background of the key players in the room, google it.
- **Being friendly and kind to everyone.** This matters more than you know. And if you are rude to the assistant or the parking lot person, believe me — the executives will find out about it.
- **Keeping mean remarks and gossip to yourself.** Don't dish. You never know who's listening. Never say anything about anyone that you would not say to their face.

- **Being gracious.** Write thank-you notes. Remember people's names. Forgive everyone everything.
- **Dressing up a little bit.** Costumes matter. Be intentional in your wardrobe. If you dress schlumpy, people will treat you like you're schlumpy. If you look like you've paid some attention to your ensemble, people will know you respect yourself, and might be more inclined to respect you themselves. You don't need to spend a lot of money to wear things that fit and are in good repair.
- **Not complaining.** If you need something, make a considered request. Otherwise, learn to suffer in silence.
- **Praising yourself.** I know you're not supposed to toot your own horn, but really — where has all this not tooting gotten you? Find graceful ways to tell stories in which you highlight your amazingness. Keep track of your sales, your positive encounters, your good reviews, etc., and make those numbers known. Be sure to bring them in for your next performance review. Let's make sure it's not just the squeaky wheels that get greased, yes?
- **Solving problems whenever you can.** If there's anything you can do to make someone's job easier, do it. Even if it's outside your area.
- **Paying attention to your body language.** Don't slouch or stare off into space or make your phone the sole object of your attention. Look alive and happy to be there.
- **Keeping your sense of humor.** Work is tough, and a good laugh — even a nice smile — can make the whole day better for you and for everyone around you.
- **Being nice.** Across all industries, I notice that being a nice person matters. Not fake nice — genuinely

nice. And remember that "nice" does not mean namby-pamby. You can be nice and have laser-sharp insights, or be nice and sarcastic, or nice and hilarious, or nice and a bit off your rocker.

If you can manage to be a nice person who is also good at solving problems, then you are on the fast track to success.

If you can be a nice person who is good at solving problems, shows up on time and prepared, doesn't gripe, and has a good sense of humor — congratulations, you are about to be promoted.

And if you aren't being promoted (or at least appreciated), it's time to go somewhere where they'll treat you like the treasure you are.

## 15-Minute Experiment

Spend 15 minutes calculating one of your personal metrics of success. Maybe you were on time for everything every day this month or didn't let the junk mail pile up. Maybe you returned every email within 24 hours. Maybe you spruced up your appearance or broke out of some other rut. Maybe you reduced churn or created a new reporting system that everyone loves. For extra points, make this success known to someone who matters.

## What If...

What if you dressed up a bit today?

# 34

# "But Work Needs Me!"

"I can't possibly take any time for myself — my work needs me!"

I hear this all the time.

"This is a really busy time of year for us…"
"We're kind of short-staffed right now…"
"I've got a weekly meeting at that time…"
"We're supposed to leave at 5 p.m., but I'm never out of there until at least 6 p.m.…."

STOP IT.

Let me speak as a business owner here. Granted, I am the owner of a very small business, but I am in an elite minority in terms of my success. I've been in business for 15 years. According to the Bureau of Labor Statistics, approximately 20 percent of small businesses fail within their first year. The failure rate increases to 30 percent by the end of the second year, 50 percent by the fifth year, and 70 percent by the tenth year. Only 4 percent of businesses the size of mine make over $250,000 in annual revenue, which I have done every year since I began — and quite a bit more some years. And this isn't factoring in the fact that mine is a woman-owned business, which, sadly, makes the odds of my success even less likely.

Here's what I want to say:

If you work for me, I want you as healthy, strong, and happy as you can be. I want your work environment to be cheerful and supportive. I want you fed, rested, and creatively fulfilled.

I would so much rather have you start your workday an hour later, having had time for a snuggle, a good breakfast, a nice walk, and 15 minutes of you working on whatever matters most to you than have you arrive earlier but all stressed-out.

And as the business owner, I do not want to be emotionally responsible for you. So if you tell me, "Hey, my parent is sick, so I'm going to need to extend the deadline on some of these less-urgent projects and keep a more flexible schedule for the next month or two," I say, "Fine. Work it out with the rest of your team. Let me know how I can help." That is much better for me than you trying to soldier on, leaving me in the dark as to why you keep dropping balls.

If you're sick, I want you to go to the doctor and rest until you feel better. Don't come in when you're unwell, thus making yourself even more tired and probably not doing any good work, anyway.

If you're in need of a vacation, I want you to cover your tasks and obligations and go for as long as you want. Send me a postcard. Enjoy yourself.

You may think I'm living in a dream world, but I had lots of jobs and gigs before I started my business, and I was always able to negotiate the terms of my employment to accommodate last-minute auditions and jobs.

Here's the trick: if you can demonstrate to your boss that you consistently earn or save the company three to ten times what they are paying you annually, you can ask for whatever you want. Show them how your excellent customer service skills cause people to spend XYZ percent more. Or how your efficiency has saved the business XYZ hours of labor costs. Or how your entertaining and informative emails cut meeting time by three hours a week.

And, since we have a moment here, let's talk about this: The opportunity costs of meetings are ridiculous. If you save your business three hours of meeting time a week, that can mean a savings of over $22,500 a year. It's a fun math game: I'm assuming an average salary of $60,000 and 2,000 working hours in a year (50 full-time weeks — I'm including some holiday time off). That makes average hourly wage around $30. If there are five people in a meeting for an hour, that's $150. Three meetings a week is $450 per week, and 50 weeks of that is $22,500. And those are just regular meetings with people who are actually in the office. Imagine when you start flying people in for meetings, plus catering costs, plus all the time that is not being spent on work that matters.

I get a little wrought up about this, because so many people spend so much valuable time in meetings, and so rarely are those meetings productive. My most popular LinkedIn Learning course is called "How to Stop Wasting Time in Meetings," and if the response I get to that training is any indication, bad meeting culture is the Dementor's Kiss of businesses everywhere. #endofrant

Showing your boss (or yourself) just how valuable you are may take some documentation work on your part, but if it can get you some extra time off or a permanent four-day workweek, it will be well worth it.

And if your boss doesn't feel this way, I bet you can either help them see the light or move on to greener pastures.

If you are self-employed, an artist, or an entrepreneur, you have even more opportunity to leverage your time. Keep track of which of your daily activities are revenue generating (like reaching out to re-enroll former clients, having sales calls, cultivating relationships with affiliate partners, and so on) and see how you can arrange your schedule to do more of those.

Go where you're celebrated; don't stay where you're tolerated. Do what brings you money and joy; hire out the rest.

## 15-Minute Experiment

Spend 15 minutes thinking about what metrics — that is to say, actual, verifiable numbers — you could use to demonstrate your worth to your boss or to your own clients. And look not only to the obvious ones, like revenue and expenses, but also more intangible ones: Are customers happier when you are there? Do the other employees bitch less and get more done when you are on the floor? Have you saved your clients or students time, money, energy, or frustration?

For 15 minutes a day for a week, play around with the question, "How have I consistently added value to the business?" and see if you don't have (1) enough data to convince your boss to give you more autonomy, a raise, or some other coveted perk, (2) enough data to go find a better job, or (3) enough confidence to double, triple, or even 10x* your pricing.

## *What If...*

What if you mentioned your progress to someone unexpected today?

---

\* My editor informs me that the word for "multiply by ten" is *decuple*. #shewiththebestvocabularywins

# 35

# When to Quit

One of the questions I like to ask people is, "What advice would the you of today like to give the you of five years ago?"

You probably won't be surprised to hear that most people would like to go back and encourage themselves to take the leap sooner. To quit that job, get out of that relationship, follow that passion, and quit believing that sacrificing their happiness is going to somehow make everything better for everyone else.

But we've all made the mistake of staying too long in a not-great situation.

Loyalty to the point of self-neglect is not helpful to anyone.

And the psychology of "sunk costs" is hard for us to wrap our heads around, much less overcome.

"Sunk costs" are how economists refer to investments of time, energy, and money that you are not getting back, no matter what, so they should be excluded from your decision-making. In other words, just because you've been married for 10 years is no reason to stay married, and just because you've spent the past five years and tens of thousands of dollars in tuition working on a PhD that you no longer care about is no reason to stick around and finish the PhD. After all, you're not getting that time or money back, so you might as well proceed forward with alacrity. Get yourself to someplace better, sooner.

Here are some questions you might ask yourself if you are thinking about quitting a job, relationship, living situation, or other enterprise that is not as fulfilling as you might like:

1. Knowing what you know now, would you do it all again?
2. If the situation never improves, do you still want to stay?
3. Does it hurt? Or is it just hard?
4. What are the reasons you think you should stay? Do those reasons reflect your values, or is it someone else's voice in your head?
5. What are the reasons you think you should go? Do those reasons reflect your values, or is it someone else's voice in your head?
6. Is the problem you're having one that money alone could solve?
7. Is the problem you're having one that a better staff or team could solve?
8. If you had quit this situation six months ago, what would be different now?
9. If you had quit this situation six months ago and now you saw someone else succeeding at it, how would you feel? (Or: If you left your spouse six months ago, and now saw them happily dating someone else, how might you feel?)
10. Which of your values are at play?
11. What does this situation remind you of?
12. If you decide to stay, how are you going to behave differently so that you can get a different result?
13. If you decide to leave, how are you going to behave differently so that you can get a different result?

## 15-Minute Experiment

Make a 90-second doodle about how you are feeling currently about the situation you'd like to quit. Remember — this is not in any way meant to be art. No one will ever see it. Just try to scribble down the shape, the feeling, the colors, the stick figures that convey your current emotional state.

Next, make another 90-second doodle about how you would *like* to be feeling.

Perhaps these two images, side by side, have some important new information for you?

## *What If...*

What if you could accurately predict the future and it looked very good for all concerned?

## 36

# Clear, Gentle, Honest, and Kind

Poor communication has done more to ruin jobs, relationships, and your personal productivity than, I believe, almost any other factor.

How often has a relationship stayed stuck because no one knew what to say?
How often has a career stalled out because someone didn't know how to ask for what they wanted?
How often has a minor situation turned into a major problem because no one addressed it soon enough?

I've watched people stew for years just because they couldn't figure out the words they needed. Or they thought that communicating strong emotions had to involve yelling or crying. Remembering that even the rockiest conversations can have moments of levity, joy, and deep appreciation for the other person can smooth the path.

Here are a few of my favorite communication tricks for opening doors, keeping your cool, and asking for what you want.

### Tips for Hard Conversations

Try approaching the person in question and asking this: "Hi. Is now an OK time for us to have a conversation that I really wish we didn't have to have?"

The beauty of this question is:

1. It gives the person you're talking to a heads-up.
2. It gives them the freedom to say, "Sure — let's talk now," or, "Can we talk after 2 p.m.?"
3. It lets them know that you're not crazy about having to do this, either.

That last bit — how it lets them know that you don't really want to have a hard talk, either — is brilliant, because it reminds both of you that you are on the same team. *The only way to have successful conversations is to be on the same team.* Even the most contentious conversation can have a basis of "You and I both want the same thing: we want for this to be resolved quickly, preferably without yelling."

For couples this is especially important, because it reframes me-against-you arguments into us-against-the-problem conversations focused on solutions.

So it's me and you, together against the fact that my mother is coming to visit.

It's me and you together against the fact that the living room is a mess.

It's me and you together against the fact that your schedule is crazy.

Or more likely: It's me and you against the fact that my mother is coming, the living room is a mess, your schedule is crazy, and we haven't had sex in ages. Best practice is to just tackle one issue at a time, though.

This you-and-me-together thing can also work wonders with customer service people, airline representatives, stingy bosses,

loud neighbors, and anyone else with whom you need to negotiate. Approaching the conversation with the attitude that
you both want the same thing — an easy resolution to whatever the problem is — means that you don't have to be mad
at them. My experience is that people are a lot more helpful
when you are kind and understanding and not mad at them. In
fact, they often come up with better solutions.

Another way to approach a potentially adversarial moment is
to ask, "What would you do if you were me?" This question has
the immediate psychological effect of them putting themselves
in your shoes, and hence, on the same side.

Here's one more negotiating trick: Remember that everyone
always thinks they are right. And you will get a lot further a lot
faster if you simply agree with them.

Whatever anyone says, try agreeing with them first. You don't
have to think they are right; you just have to agree that they
think they are right. So if they are saying that "XYZ politician
is the best candidate," or that "Pizza with pineapple is the most
delicious," and you vehemently disagree, try responding with
something simple, like "That's cool that you think that," or just
nod and say, "OK," without eye-rolling.

Few things are as disarming as being agreed with, and the fact
of the matter is, to them, their version of events is correct. Their
version of events does not have to match your version of events
in order for you to agree with them, you know? If they are saying that they "always take out the trash," well, that's what feels
real to them. And even if you know that you personally took
out the trash twice last week, it costs you nothing to say, "Yes.
You have done great work in trash removal. I appreciate that."
Agreement calms them down; plus, it reminds you that there's

more than one version of the truth, and that's a great way to start to come to a mutually satisfying decision.

## Intrapersonal Communication

You have also suffered when you are not on the same side as yourself. You need to be on your own team, first and foremost.

Do whatever it takes to reduce or eliminate the negative chatter in your mind. There's about a grillion books about how to do this, but you can also try meditation, hypnosis, exercise, prayer — whatever works for you.

I have recently been experimenting with how to be critical of myself without being self-critical. In other words, I've been taking long, hard, questioning looks at my life, my decisions, and my work *without* immediately sinking into self-loathing. It's like I'm a kindly teacher, looking over my work and saying, "Good job. What could you have done better, hon?" And then answering that question for myself as honestly as I can. S'fun.

Your body is the only home you have, and your mind is the only one you get, and you don't have either of them for very long, so practice being good to yourself, OK?

## 15-Minute Experiment

Do 15 minutes' worth of journaling about how it feels — or how it might feel — to value serenity, alignment, and cooperation over being "right."

## What If...

What if you never needed to be right ever again?

# 37

# Health and Ill Health

The world sometimes acts as though ill health is a moral failing. Like, if you were truly a good person, you would be young and vibrant and slim and laughing your whole life long.

The fact is, everyone is dealing with something healthwise. If it's not your health you're worried about, it's someone else's. And much of disease is environmental, genetic, or otherwise out of your control. So step one is: give yourself a break. Quit being mad at yourself for having mood disorders, food sensitivities, chronic disease, stress-related disorders, genetic abnormalities, or whatever it is you've got.

And maybe quit being mad at your beloveds for getting sick, too.

Health and wellness issues are a true test of your spiritual development. After all, it's easy to be grateful when everything's going well, isn't it? But when your body and mind are suffering — and it all feels so *personal* — it's suddenly a lot harder to keep small-mindedness, jealousy, and ingratitude at bay. I mean, what if you don't want to be a "brave cancer warrior"? What if you want to whine and cry and complain?

Spiritually mature people recognize that "bravery means never complaining" is a fallacy, and that crying doesn't reflect weakness or a lack of faith. Spiritually mature people trust themselves to have whatever feelings they are having, because they know that feelings are fleeting.

Here is a story about me:

I have always lived with depression and anxiety, even when I was a kid and "childhood depression" was not a thing. They just said I was "often sad" and "too sensitive." In the late '90s, my good friend Charlie recommended I read Andrew Solomon's work of towering genius, *The Noonday Demon*, which is a brilliant book about depression, and I realized that I was not, in fact, "too sensitive" — I was depressed and always had been. I scampered off and got myself a therapist and some medication, and since then life's been better — not perfect, but definitely less agonizing.

So that's the backdrop.

Now, as it happens, I have always had dense breasts. (Insert your own joke here.) Almost every mammogram I've ever had, they've wanted to follow up with a second mammogram or with an ultrasound. The first time they wanted to give me an ultrasound, the appointment was two weeks away. I agreed to the appointment, and then promptly put it out of my mind.

When I mentioned it at lunch to an easily agitated friend, her eyes got big. "Aren't you worried sick? I'd be losing sleep if it were me!" I said no — that I refused to worry about something that hadn't happened yet. And sure enough, the ultrasound came back normal. I was so glad I hadn't spent any of my precious life energy fretting over something that was nothing.

Over the years, this routine got repeated. But then, one day early in 2020, instead of it being nothing, the doctor thought it might be something and wanted to biopsy. He looked me in the eye* and said, "We can see something, but we're not sure what it is. And since we're not sure, I want to do a biopsy." He took a breath. "I'm sure this is very scary and stressful for you —"

I cut him off. "This is not scary or stressful for me, because I'm 99 percent sure that it's nothing. And if it turns out that it is not nothing, then we'll deal with that then."

"Oh," he said, a bit taken aback, but smiling. "Good attitude."

I laughed and said, "Well, sometimes, decades of personal development work can really come in handy."

As it turned out, it wasn't nothing. I had a touch of the cancer.

I had a very common, tiny, slow-growing tumor — "indolent" was the word my oncological surgeon used, and it made me laugh that I got lazy cancer. It was removed in an outpatient surgery, and then I had five days of twice-daily radiation treatments. I was especially fortunate because, thanks to President Obama, I had health insurance, and because I was living near Santa Barbara, California, there was a big, brand-new cancer treatment center with top-of-the-line everything.†

Honestly, while I can't say I loved the experience, it didn't affect me much, and I didn't tell very many people that it was even happening. I actually forgot to tell my mom about it.

Ten weeks later, I sustained a stress fracture just above my ankle. It was slow to heal, and after hobbling around for a

---

\* Have they given doctors additional training about eye contact in recent years? I feel like overall, healthcare providers are way more sensitive than they used to be, and their communication skills have really stepped up. Or maybe I've just been lucky. Either way: Well done, practitioners!

† Hint: If you're going to get sick, do it where the rich people live.

month or so, I was finally put into a big plaster cast for another six weeks. Frankly, it still hurts.

Six weeks after that, one of my closest, dearest, most wonderful friends died of cancer. I am still grieving. We all are.

A month later, my father's lung cancer, which had been in re-mission, returned, and with the blessings of his doctors at the VA (and God bless the VA), he decided he didn't want to pursue any further treatment. They suggested he had a few months left. We got to work moving him to the town where my sister lived and helping him make his end-of-life preparations.

Then my cat got very sick (and very expensive) and died. I was devastated.

Then I had to move out of the apartment building I'd been living in for the past 10 years that I loved with my entire being. Even though it was tiny and outdated, I absolutely adored its old turquoise Formica and plain '50s-style kitchen cabinets. Plus, it was across from an estuary, so there were always egrets and herons and even a local roadrunner to watch. I could watch the sun set over the mountains from my desk, and I could walk barefoot to the most perfect beach and stroll and swim, which I did almost every day, regardless of the weather. Seriously — it was the best apartment in the world. Anyway, the building got sold and, thanks to a loophole in the city code, the new landlord was able to kick Luke and me out and turn it into a short-term rental property. I was devastated and furious. I wrote letters to the mayor and the vice mayor and the city council, and I contacted four different lawyers... all of whom suggested I start packing.

We tried to buy a house, but everything was way out of our price range.* Even rentals were astronomical.

---

* This would be the downside of living where all the rich people live.

Did I mention this was all during the Covid lockdown? Yeah — Covid started just a month or two before my breast cancer diagnosis. So that was happening.

We scrambled to find a new place to live, and then scrambled to afford the higher rent of the new place. I felt grateful that my little business could support all these financial hits and that my work was flexible enough that I could manage all this change and uncertainty with some ease.

Then, despite being double-vaccinated and boosted and masked and in a "pod" and pretty darn cautious all the way around, I got Covid, and never got better. (I know — riiiiiight?? Take a breath. We'll get through this.) Like an estimated 5 to 10 percent of people who get Covid, I got what is commonly known as long-haul Covid.

I want to take a moment to say a bit more about long-haul Covid, because it's governed much of my life since January 2021, and there's a good chance someone you know has it, too.

Long-haul Covid is, as of this writing, a medical mystery with no known cure. It is actually a collection of overlapping syndromes and symptoms, and it shows up differently in different people. This means that some people don't know they have it, and some doctors aren't even convinced that it's a real thing.

Let me assure you, it is a very, very, very real thing.

The main known symptoms are, alphabetically:

anxiety
brain fog
chest pain
chronic cough

chronic pain

depression

extreme fatigue

gastrointestinal issues

heart palpitations

joint pain

loss of sexual desire

loss of taste and/or smell

ME/CFS — myalgic encephalomyelitis / chronic fatigue syndrome: Another complicated, understudied, and hard-to-diagnose syndrome mostly defined by extreme fatigue and unrefreshing sleep but also affecting other systems in the body

migraines

PEM — post-exertional malaise: Charming term, right? Should come with its own bottle-green velvet fainting couch. It's when a small amount of exertion or exercise causes you to completely collapse. So if I lift a heavy box, I'll be in bed for a day or two. The latest research I've seen indicates that there seems to be some kind of misfunction in the mitochondria, so instead of exercise breaking down your muscles and then building them back up again (which is how you get stronger) PEM causes the muscles to *only* break down, thus making you weaker. Whatever the science turns out to be, the fact that I can't work out at all or even take a nice long walk is absolutely punishing.

POTS — postural orthostatic tachycardia syndrome: A dysfunction of the autonomic nervous system. As nearly as I can make out, it means that when you stand up, your nervous system doesn't signal

to send more blood flow to your heart, lungs, and
brain, so you get dizzy, lightheaded, and short of
breath.*
shortness of breath
thirst

This is only a partial list of symptoms. Long-haul Covid can
affect nearly every tissue and organ in the body.

I'm hoping that by the time you are reading this, long-haul
is long gone and this will all seem almost charmingly archaic
and easy to fix. "Remember when we didn't have a cure for
long-haul? Or even an accurate way to diagnose it? Ha, ha,
ha — what a lark!"

But for now...if anyone ever says, "Hey, would you like an
incurable, long-term illness?" just say no. Even if they offer you
something really nifty in exchange.

It's almost funny to think back to when I had a schedule
crammed with a bunch of part-time jobs and gigs and was
always running to auditions and rehearsals and shows — I remember thinking that I would give almost anything just to
have a day to spend in bed. And now I spend a great deal of my
time in bed and have fantasies about being able to run errands,
go visit with friends, or go for a walk. Always greener, right?

Here are ten things that make my life not as bad as it might
be otherwise:

1.  I am extremely fortunate that my family and friends
    are loving and reliable and adore me even when I'm
    an incoherent mess.

---

\* It's also a fun tongue-twister and vocal warm-up for those of you who are
always looking for unusual things to say. Try it: *postural orthostatic tachycar-*
*dia syndrome!* You're welcome.

2. I work from home and I am my own boss, so I can adjust my schedule as needed.

3. The cats think it's great that I've finally caught on to the whole "sleep for 12 to 14 hours a day" thing.

4. I ended up moving to Connecticut to be near my sister and her family. I found a wonderful 1958 ranch house with no stairs. Stairs kill me. Living in this house means I can enjoy the whole place, including the back deck, where the birdsong is so delicious — it's like I live inside a meditation CD.

5. I may feel crappy, but I am not in any real pain. This is an incalculable blessing.

6. At least some of my income is "passive" from television residuals and book royalties and such, so even though my ability to earn may have dropped a bit, I can still pay my bills.*

7. I can write from bed. I'm doing it now. See?

8. One of the seldom-sung benefits of *not* being a member of the Happy Childhood Club is that I have an amazing ability to compartmentalize. I can ignore all kinds of physical, psychic, and emotional hurt when I need to. Also, I have a very high tolerance for discomfort and am stubborn as fuck. So when I need to suck it up and keep going, I do.

9. Two words: online shopping.

10. A lifetime in the theater taught me something called "performance energy," which means that when it comes time for me to teach a class online or deliver a virtual keynote, or if I have a consulting gig, I can slap on a believable smile and act like a perfectly healthy

---

* For now, anyway.

person. Weasels could be gnawing off my knees beneath my desk, and I would still deliver a hell of a show. It doesn't matter how exhausted or sick I feel — if it's time for me to work, I can suit up and show up and give 100 percent. Then the weasels and I go back to bed and collapse.

I tell you all this to say that even though it's been a two-year period jam-packed with loss, suffering, surgery, pain, grief, dislocation, heartbreak, and chronic illness, I am not unhappy.

My prayers of gratitude are just as sincere as ever. And not in a Little Mary Sunshine kind of way. I'm not sugarcoating anything or pretending that anything is better than it is. I am genuinely grateful.

Why? Because I focus on what I can control, which is my outlook. My attitude. My prayer and meditation practice. My relationships.

Consider these little nuggets:

- If you focus on the circumstances that are outside your control, you will always be unhappy.
- Learn to be as realistic as you can be in your pain/ unwellness assessments — but don't let it mean anything.
- Neither exaggerate nor minimize (except for comic effect).
- Going to get that exam, that test, that annual physical is a true act of courage. Please stop psyching yourself out. I know, it's awful and a terrible system and they probably can't help you much anyway, but still — go. OK?

## 15-Minute Experiment

Take a deep breath and make the appointment with the doctor or healing practitioner you've been putting off. Then reward yourself with something delightful.

## *What If...*

What if you remembered that you can do hard things?

# 38

# Micro-Blessings

We dream of the big things that we think will make us happy: a new house, a boat, an extended vacation.... But I notice that it is the little things that make life joyful. And, let's face it, little things are easier to come by than big things.

I like to think of these little daily pops of joy as micro-blessings.

Micro-blessings are the little things that boost your mood, restore your spirit, and cause that delightful little smile that reaches all the way to the crinkles of your eyes.

Some micro-blessings are free, others cost money. Some are fleeting, while others are longer-lasting. Here's my list — but please, make your own list, won't you?

> Good undies
> Connecting with a friend you can be vulnerable with
> A good pen (I swoon for good pens)
> Bread and butter
> Peonies
> Finding $20 hidden in a pocket
> A freshly made bed with lovely, clean cotton sheets
> A well-tuned guitar
> Birdsong
> Comfortable shoes
> The color of the sky just before dawn
> All dogs
> A cool cloth when you're fevered

A warm compress when you're hurt
Geraniums
Shea butter cream for dry skin
Unexpected compliments
A bath
Remembering all the words to a theme song from a
     TV program from when you were young
The affection of an animal friend
A favorite song on the radio
A puddle reflecting a cloud
Swimming
A lemon
Fresh towels
Making funny faces with babies and young children in
     line at the grocery store
Hummingbirds
Healthy flirtation
First stretch of the day
Meadow flowers
A cup of tea with milk and a slightly inappropriate
     amount of sugar

## 15-Minute Experiment

Start your own list of your favorite micro-blessings today, and
see how many more you can find in the next few days. Think of
it as a very practical "gratitude practice." Give yourself one as
a reward when you do something hard. Ask your friends and
colleagues for theirs. Make a practice of remembering someone else's and doing one for or with them.

## What If...

What if you found profound joy in the simplest things?

# 39

# Intermezzo: Drop

drop drop drop
drop what you have been holding
drop the idea that you are confused
drop the idea that you are broke
drop the idea that there is any part of you that is unlovable or
    unnecessary

drop it
set it down
set your burden down
set down your grief
set down your aloneness
set down your stubbornness

sit down on the side of the road
set your bundles down next to you
like cats just sit there
don't do
don't rush
don't have a thought
feel your heartbeat
feel the breath go in and out of you
feel how you are supported in this very moment

there is nothing you need that you don't have in this very
    moment
there is nothing that is not possible for you

don't do
don't rush
stop thinking
be…

be on the side of the road
set your burdens down

you can pick them back up later
just set them down for now

set down your identity
set down your desire to be liked
set down the frantic need to be approved of
set down the idea that there is any lack or absence or shortage
    of anything anywhere

feel your heart beat
feel your breath
feel the air on your skin
feel gravity

stop fighting

we love you and you're doing great
let your hands be loose
stay don't wander
stay don't rush to answers
stay in this moment
stay in not knowing

feel the forgiveness for not knowing
it's like a rain comes down and washes the dust off you
you are warm and safe

you are needed and loved
you are perfect whole and complete
there is nothing wrong with you

and your ego will fight that
do you see it throwing its little tantrum
you say "I love you ego, you are loved and you're doing great"

so together we gather in this circle
sitting down by the side of the road
with our burdens and our stories and our excuses
the same 57 negative thoughts
that we have been thinking since we were twelve
we have set aside for now

you seek transformation
you are in the place of transformation
you seek a new life
you are in the place of a new life
you can relax
you've made it
congratulations you found it
you can stay like this

this is the real world
this is the real world

• • •

To watch a video of this improvised poem/blessing and download your own copy, go here: 15MinuteMethod.com/bonus.

# 40

# Rehearsing Calm

We know that overwhelm is not an outside problem, because we see people who work in chronically overwhelming conditions. There they are — in a constant crisis situation — and yet they remain calm, cool, and capable.

ER staff. Animal rescuers. First responders. Firefighters. Airline gate attendants when a flight has been canceled. People who clear out hoarder homes. People in war zones.

Call to mind an image of one of those workers. What do you see?

You see them moving at a steady pace, being respectful of others. They are not yelling or freaking out. They have a process, and they are sticking to it. They are unmoved by your emotions. They are doing everything they can to make the situation better, all the while knowing that improvement may not be possible.

They are entirely aware that death, tragedy, and misfortune are daily occurrences. And it's not that they are unfeeling — quite the contrary — but they keep their attention on what they can do in that moment to help. They don't exaggerate. They don't globalize. They don't make it someone else's fault. Most impressively, they often have an excellent sense of humor.

God bless those people for showing us how to be present, compassionate, and centered. How to work at the best of our ability, even when the world is collapsing around us.

Sometimes being genuinely helpful means saying, "No," or, "Wait your turn."

This is why we call them heroes. Because they demonstrate leadership when the rest of us are broken and helpless.

How do they do it? Well, for one, they know their business. They are experts. They practice over and over again. Firefighters perform drills. Flight attendants repeat the rules about the emergency exits over and over again so that *we* are drilled in how to behave. It's not that they think we haven't heard it before. It's that they know that in the event of an emergency, humans do not rise to a new level of excellence, but rather revert to their level of preparation.

This is why performers have rehearsals. And, tragically, why schools have active shooter drills.

So often, you lead yourself into overwhelm by imagining the worst possible outcome. You, tripping over your words during the presentation. You, wearing a ridiculous outfit to the fancy party. You, alone and abandoned and broke because you spoke your mind.

This is not you using your imaginative powers for good.

Why not rehearse excellence?
Why not rehearse calm?
Why not practice remaining open and gracious in the face of criticism?

## 15-Minute Experiment

Think about a circumstance that stresses you out. Maybe being asked to present at a meeting or having to give a speech? Or maybe flying? Or being barked at by a big dog?

Make a 90-second doodle about how that circumstance makes you feel. As usual, feel free to just use colors and shapes and stick figures — you're simply trying to express the feeling so you can understand it better. And then make another 90-second doodle about how you would like it to feel.

Let these two drawings inform your decision to take a quick, easily affordable action step to build more calm confidence in that stressful circumstance. Maybe watch a TED Talk about public speaking or spend 15 minutes hanging out at the local dog park. Take that step today, and if it works — keep going!

## What If...

What if you keep in mind that you have done impossible things before? Right?

# 41

# Calm While under Attack

Many years ago I was hosting a large three-day event that was all about helping creative people become successful entrepreneurs. I created an agenda that was a beautiful blend of practical training and careful inner work. We had over a hundred people fly in from all over the US and the world,* and it was wonderfully exciting.

But there were two rotten apples in the bunch — two friends who took it upon themselves to point out everything that they didn't care for. They griped and complained endlessly. They pointed out every way in which they disagreed with me. And while my team and I are always grateful for well-intentioned advice and even harsh criticism, it was obvious that these two and their crappy attitude were throwing the whole event off-balance.

The morning of the second day, one of them — let's call her Debbie — came to the mic and started to rip me to pieces over something that had happened the day before.† I said

---

\*   Peru! Israel! New Zealand! For the girl who never had a successful birthday party as a kid, it was a thrill to welcome these visitors.

†   This story gets even weirder when I tell you what she was mad about: I had offered the room the opportunity to donate money to help build schools in sub-Saharan Africa. She said she felt "blindsided" by the presentation. She was indignant because she felt the hard conditions that were being reported by the charity in question "wasn't the real Africa." She thought it was "irresponsible" of me to ask for donations from the people in the room. We raised over $15,000.

something like, "Yes — OK. I hear you. I get it. Thank you for sharing. It's time to move on." I remember watching the blood rise in her face as she persisted in her attack, and I began to slow my breathing. As her sarcastic, demeaning tone intensified, I felt my feet root more firmly into the floor. I maintained eye contact with her. I remember holding out one arm and pulling the other one back a bit, almost as if I were going to embrace her, so as to direct her energy exclusively toward me — I didn't want anyone else to feel the effect of her poison. My team leader said that from the back of the room, it looked as though I were Artemis, drawing back her bow. (Isn't that a great image?)

I did not explain myself, nor did I apologize. I said I understood that she had strong feelings about what had happened, and while I would be happy to have a private conversation with her, we were not going to continue this dialogue now.

Shortly after this exchange, it was time for a break, and while I normally go backstage during breaks so I can rest and gather my energy for the next teaching, I knew that this time it was important that I stay in the room. As I walked around the tables, I was very touched by how many of the participants let me know how much they disagreed with Debbie, and how rude and wrong they found her. I appreciated their support, and the old adage about how nothing draws a group of people together faster than a common dislike of someone else was absolutely proved again. Debbie had actually done me a favor with her tirade — she made everyone else in the room jump to my defense. Bless her heart.

Here's the most important part: As I was circulating, being reassuring and reassured, a woman in her early 30s came up to me with tears in her eyes. "That was amazing," she said. "I have lived my entire life terrified of being criticized, and to see you up there, being so calm and gracious in the face of such…I've never seen that before. This changes everything for me —" And at this point she broke off, tears streaming down her face. I gave her a big hug, and I thought to myself, "OK — if I had to deal with a bit of upset in order for this woman to receive the lesson that it is possible to be criticized and not crumble, then it was all worthwhile."

How was I able to keep my cool while under attack? Several thousand hours of stage experience in my back pocket mean that I feel safest onstage. Several thousand hours of teaching experience helped, too.

I also know that sometimes doing deep work with people can bring up strong feelings, and if a person is not emotionally mature enough to handle it, they may lash out to release some of the internal pressure they are feeling.

Finally, I was acutely aware that as the host and leader of the event, I was "mommy." I was setting the tone for everyone, and it was imperative that I model good behavior. The pressure of leadership caused me to "pull up" and to prioritize the overall well-being of the room over my own feelings.

Helpful tip: Sometimes when people become emotionally upset, but they were raised in an environment in which they were not allowed to express their feelings, they will start complaining about other things. The air-conditioning is too high. Their chair is too hard. The coffee is too bitter. They express their discomfort as a physical problem rather than an emotional one. This is why I've seen smart leaders and canny salespeople offer blankets, water pitchers on every table, frequent snacks, and other creature comforts.

During that break, my team let Debbie and her friend know that since this event was obviously not a good fit for them, we would be cheerfully refunding their ticket price, and they were cordially invited to leave. Which they did, with no additional drama.

That night I cried. A lot. And then I got up the next day and showed up with a smile. It turned out to be one of the most successful and profitable events I've ever had.

## 15-Minute Experiment

Consider how you respond to criticism, or how you behave when someone else is wrong. Can you imagine just taking in what is being said without defending yourself or launching a counterattack? Could you just let someone be wrong without correcting them — even if the thing they are wrong about is *you*? Consider that you can be responsive without being reactive. In other words, you can take a breath and respond to them without feeling victimized and without heightened emotion. Practice calling up this calm whenever you feel stressed-out today.

On the other hand, if you tend to shut down in the face of conflict or disagreement, you may want to practice taking a deep breath and speaking your truth.

## What If...

What if you pretended you were a member of the royal family and followed the maxim of "never complain and never explain"?

# 42

# Be Amazed. Be Very, Very Amazed.

You might be noticing that as you have implemented the 15-Minute Method, other people have — astonishingly — begun to change, too.

### The Mysterious Power of Changing Your Patterns

The intractable boss has become more flexible.
The perfectionist assistant has developed a sense of humor.
And even the family seems to be more relaxed and having more fun.

When you change how you are, you give others room to change how they are.

And when you are focused on that over which you have control (as opposed to things over which you have zero control, like other people) you tend to be more peaceful. Also, you are less argumentative, victim-y, or nitpicky, which also makes others nicer.

You have created what we call a virtuous cycle, which is the opposite of a vicious cycle. You start focusing on the good in your life, and suddenly you perceive more good in your life, which makes you calmer and more joyful, which makes other people calmer and more joyful, which creates more good in your life.

## Avoiding Backsliding and the
## Seductive Allure of Old Patterns

You may not know that when you create a new habit, you are overwriting your old habit, neurologically speaking. Which means the neural pattern of the old habit is still there. So if you stop doing the new habit, what happens? You fall right back into the old habit. The original programming wins. This is why chronic dieters and lottery winners so often end up right back where they started: despite new circumstances, they fail to permanently replace the habits that created the problem in the first place.

So if anything that you've started doing is working for you, please keep at it. Maybe get a buddy to support you. For years, the only reason I worked out regularly was because my friend was meeting me there, and I didn't want to let her down. Social accountability is an excellent tool. Think of it as positive peer pressure.

## New Challenges (aka "New Level, New Devil")

Notice how you have created a new world for yourself. Guess what comes with it? New problems.

And new problems always feel worse than old problems, because we do not know their size, shape, or duration. The unfamiliar problem is actually a great blessing, but it takes some serious spiritual maturity to recognize it as such.

For example, you've worked hard at your side hustle, and you're ready to do it full-time. But where you once had the problem of "How do I squeeze in time for my side hustle?" now you have the problem of "I am my own boss, so how do I structure my time?" And you may have the problem of hiring and training team members, dealing with scaling up, and holding on while riding the roller coaster of entrepreneurship. Now, these are excellent problems to have, but they feel scarier than your old problems and are challenging you in a new way.

Congratulations! Your new fears are a great sign of growth! YAY!

## 15-Minute Experiment

Spend time answering these questions:

1. How has your life changed lately?
2. What new problems are you facing?
3. Where are you being called to grow?
4. Can you feel some pride in, and fascination with, your new problems?
5. Is there a song you want to start playing to remind yourself of your overall awesomeness?

## What If...

What if you walked into every room to a soundtrack of great music and loud applause? (Go ahead and play that "walk-on" music, yes?)

## 43

# Wisdom, Courage, Justice, and Moderation (as Translated by Me)

Sometimes people come to me, concerned because they are not sure what the purpose of their life is. They ask me about finding one's life purpose.

And here's what I say:

The purpose of your life is to experience life.

The purpose of your life is to experience your life to the degree that you are able.

Becoming the best version of yourself is optional, but approved of.

So there's nothing special you need to do to fulfill your life purpose, except stay open to experiencing all the things life offers you, including hardship, heartbreak, and sorrow.

And you also get to experience the good stuff, too, right? Healing and love and sacred moments.

It's all real, and it's all equally valuable. The good stuff isn't better than the bad stuff. In fact, if you asked a Stoic, they'd say the good stuff may not even be good *or* bad, but rather something to learn from.

I have developed a long-standing love of Stoic philosophy, which, sadly, has the worst name possible. *Stoic* seems unfeeling, and *philosophy* sounds dull. But the Stoics (think Greeks and Romans from the fourth century BCE to the second century CE, like Epictetus, Seneca, and Marcus Aurelius) created what, to me anyway, are the most sensible rules for living I've ever found.

Here's my completely amateurish attempt to share a few Stoic highlights featuring their values of wisdom, courage, justice, and moderation.

### Wisdom

Embody learning — not just reading about things but trying new things and implementing them.

Learn continuously — be a lifelong learner.

Stay humble to all that you do not know — especially when it comes to someone else's life experience.

Stay humble to the mystery of life.

Know what needs to be done and what doesn't. This alone is an incredibly valuable exercise.

Always assume goodwill, but also take time to reflect on your own motives, as well as the motives of others.

Know who you are.

### Courage

Be strong of heart. Courage is not about physical bravery; it's about inner bravery: the ability to be honest with yourself and others, even when the truth doesn't flatter you; the ability to share, to embrace, to have unreasonable compassion. This is strength that matters, and it can be practiced no matter one's age, life circumstances, or condition.

Be willing to speak the truth, regardless of the consequences.

Be aware of death, without fear or regret — and without letting it decide everything. They call it memento mori, and I find a daily reminder that our time here is finite very motivating.

Make a habit of conquering fear.

Practice generosity.

## Justice

All people are created equal, so treat them that way. That means everyone.

All people (and, I think, animals) are deserving of respect, so give it to them.

Everyone holds a piece of the truth, so listen to them.

Everyone holds a piece of the divine, so revere them.

Avoid anger, revenge, jealousy, and other toxic, addictive emotions.*

## Moderation

Neither exaggerate nor minimize, except for comic effect.

---

\* Sometimes I wonder: Are people just bored? Is that why they behave so poorly? Smart people living in understimulating environments, in dehumanizing jobs, in ugly housing. Is it any wonder they rail and complain and become lethargic and furious and skeptical?

Be respectful of strong substances, strong people, and other things that might overwhelm your judgment.

Be respectful of the limited influence you have over others. You are just a background player in everyone else's life.

Set a good example.*

## 15-Minute Experiment

Take just 15 minutes to write out your own personal philosophy of life. Write swiftly. Don't ponder. Feel free to crib ideas from others, the way I did above. You can think of it as "Lessons for the Children" — what would you like to be able to teach the world's young ones? For bonus points, share it with someone you like and respect.

## What If...

What if you refrained from overcomplicating?

---

\* Those of us who have younger siblings have often been told to "set a good example." Turns out, that's excellent advice. We tend to mimic each other. So if you want everyone in your office to be prompt, respectful, good-humored, and calm, that shit starts with you. Especially if you're the boss, but even if not. Emotions are contagious.

# 44

# Affirmations to Calm Your Shit Down

The only way to change your behavior is to change your thinking. And, due to our love of habits, the only way to change your thinking is to intentionally replace old, self-sabotaging thoughts with better thoughts.

The personal development world loves "affirmations" because they are quick and easy to create, and, done properly, really can help change a person.

Affirmations are not magic incantations. If they were, then everyone with a Post-it on their mirror would be a millionaire. But they are a beneficial way to bring some poetry and self-awareness to what otherwise might be a daily litany of self-criticisms and limiting beliefs.

Here are a few I particularly like, and when I find them useful:

*I appear as this now.*

For when I feel self-critical about my age, body, or appearance.

*The road has led to here.*

For when I feel I am not yet sufficiently successful.

*I have not been brought this far to be left behind now.*

For when I feel discouraged.

*The moon is my mother. Hi, Mom!*

For when I feel alone or abandoned.

*This problem is outside my control, so I hand it over to the divine.*

When I need to remember the limits of my feeble powers.

*I refuse to worry; I pray.*

When I need to channel my concern about another person or situation into proactive energetic healing.

*Divine intelligence tells me all I need to know.*

When I find myself anxious about how something is going to go. This phrase reminds me that when I need to know more, more will be revealed.

*I'll know what I need to know when I need to know it.*

Same as above.

*Divine love flows through me, expressing itself as me.*

When I need to remember that I am the hands and feet of God.

*Divine intelligence flows through me, expressing itself as me.*

See above.

*Miracles happen every day.*

When I need to remember that just because something is unlikely doesn't mean it's impossible.

*Knowing what I know now, I would have behaved differently.*

When I need to forgive myself.

*I am a speck on a speck on a speck, and I'm here for just a moment. Let's enjoy this.*

When my ego starts getting puffy, I find it reassuring to remember my insignificance.

*This planet belongs to the sea.*

I like to remember that this planet is mostly water, and that most of the creatures in the water have no idea that humans even exist, much less have any concern for our strutting and fretting. I like to consider my life from the point of view of, say, a whale. Again, I find my insignificance, and nature's profound indifference to me, deeply comforting.

*Everything is temporary.*

Because it is.

## 15-Minute Experiment

Have fun creating some affirmations of your own. Feel free to make them funny, disrespectful, or dirty, but do see if you can make them *true*. Or at least true for you. If you find one you particularly like, you might want to put it on a mug.*

## What If...

What if the most recent meteor shower was a reminder that you are made of starstuff?

---

* FYI, you can get my "Everything Is Temporary" mug and other fun items in the shop on my website: Shop.TheRealSamBennett.com.

# 45

# Books I Haven't Written Yet

There are a few books I keep threatening to write, but I don't — mostly because the ideas are so simple, the books would only be a few pages long.

On the other hand, I probably would have said that about the idea "spend 15 minutes a day on something that matters to you," and look what that turned into.

Here are the summaries of my so-far unwritten books:

### The 3×5 Solution

I came up with this one with my dear friend Robert MacPhee, author of *Living a Values Based Life*, when we were both speaking at a conference. I, as usual, had my big stack of index cards and was taking notes and doodling and occasionally passing jokey notes to Robert. During a break, we started singing the praises of 3×5 cards and how delightfully useful they are, and finally one of us said, "If you are trying to do more in one day than you can fit on a 3×5 card, you are trying to do too much."

DING!

So that's it. Use 3×5 cards to create your to-do lists, to capture ideas, to outline home renovations or book plots or business strategies. If you start to overfill the card, you'll know you've got too many ideas or steps, and it's time to start a new card.

I've written all my books with the help of index cards. They are my secret writing-success tool. Perfect for capturing ideas on the fly. Easy to carry around, stack, rearrange, and toss out.

PS. If you're an index card snob like me and you feel aggrieved that the ones in the office supply stores have gotten so flimsy, please know that you can order "card stock" or "super sturdy" index cards online and once again experience high-quality index card joy.

## *Treat Them Like You Like Them*

This is my business book, and it contains the secret to my success in business, even though I had absolutely no training or experience as a business owner: *treat them like you like them.*

Treat your clients — current, past, and prospective — like you like them.
Treat your team members like you like them.
Treat yourself like you like you.
Treat your colleagues like you like them.
Treat your coaches, advisers, and teachers like you like them.
Treat money like you like money.
Treat your business like you like it.

Yep. That's about it.

## *Fuck Everything*

This book is for when you want to scream the title out loud. It has just one page, with just three sentences:

> Drink some water and get some sleep, OK?
> You're doing better than you think you are.
> You are loved.

## 15-Minute Experiment

Spend 15 minutes making some notes about what book you would like to write. Or what funny book titles you can come up with. Be careful, though — you may suddenly realize how easy it is to create and publish a short ebook, and then you'll be a published author! #eeeep!

## *What If...*

What if your secret superpowers are in full effect?

# 46

# Our February Forecast

You have moved from a time of learning into a
Time of testing what you know.
The moon lights your way.
Spirit is climbing up through you
From your belly; out your mouth
Causing you to speak truths you might rather not.
You cannot contain the thump of your heart's desire anymore.
Everyone sees your competence, your expertise
(Except, perhaps, you).
It's time for a new relationship with old values.
You are the authority, babe.
You are grace personified.
Hope is real.
And you may have the urge to treat this all as an intellectual
    exercise.
But darling…
You are in the midst of your life's work.
This is no time to be shy.
You are calling in the others to help.
This is no time to hold back.
Buckle up, buttercup — the change is real.


## 15-Minute Experiment

Set a timer for 15 minutes and press Start. Write out a list
of things you appreciate about yourself. Qualities, strengths,

skills — maybe some things you wish other people would see and appreciate more, maybe some things that only you know about you. Repeat yourself if you need to, but keep writing until the timer goes off.

## *What If...*

What if you made it to the top of the mountain? And you celebrated and took photos and gazed out at the far horizons? And then...you kept walking?

Welcome to your new adventure, friend.

# Acknowledgments

So many have influenced this book — overtly and covertly, visibly and invisibly, knowingly and unknowingly — I could never name them all, so let me start by thanking all the clients, students, colleagues, readers, fellow authors, and friends who have inspired, delighted, encouraged, and cared for me and my work over the years. You have no idea how much every review, endorsement, and thumbs-up matters. Please let me know when I can return the favor.

Without the guidance and unflagging cheerleading of my agent, Michele Martin, and the powerhouse team at New World Library — Georgia Hughes, Kristen Cashman, Kim Corbin, and all the other smart, caring people — this book would never have happened. I am in your debt.

I am fortunate to have a group of friends who are always inspiring me to do and be better. Special thanks to my personal Board of Geniuses: Amy Ahlers, Carol Allen, Melanie Benson, Rhonda Britten, Michael Dunn, Jeannie Esti, James Hallett, Jennifer Hardaway, Michael Kosik, Allison Lane, Sarah Laws, Melissa McFarlane, Stephanie Miller, Ed O'Neill, Andrea Owen, Jennifer Raim, Linda Sivertsen and the Beautiful Writers Group, Sarah Sullivan, Phil and Amanda Swann, Rick Tamlyn, and Margaret Weber.

Thanks to my family: Gunnar Bennett; Beatrice Briggs; Andrea, Philip, Sasha, and Foster Goetz; Laura and Will Ray; Brad Bennett; and all the Briggses in the Beehive.

Many teachers, writers, and speakers have generously shared their wisdom with me, and I am moon-and-stars grateful for their work: Sam Christensen, Greg Delson, Katie and Gay Hendricks, Sam Kaner, Byron Katie, Anne Lamott, Robert MacPhee, Elisabeth Manning, Clate Mask, Charlie and Annie McQuary, Alice Miller, Stephen Mitchell, David Neagle, Marshall B. Rosenberg, Ben Saltzman, William Thomas, Jr., Leonore Tjia, and Steph Tuss.

To the people who support my business day-to-day, I adore you madly: Lucie Balassone-Mosny, Veronica Guzzardi, and Jeremy Yanofsky. Honorable mentions to Allie Beckman, MaryKay Morgan, and TJ Slattery.

Double-extra-special thanks and love to Ron West, Stephen Ramsey, and Luke Hannington. Luke gets an extra shout-out because he composed the theme song for the audiobook version.

And special thanks to our recording engineer, Brian Johnson at Real Media.

If your name should be on this list and isn't, I am remiss, and I apologize, or I'm keeping your identity a secret to protect you from your many raving fans, of whom I am one. Obvs.

Finally, to you, the reader: my gratitude is as boundless as the sea, my love as deep.*

---

\* Phrase lifted from *The Most Excellent and Lamentable Tragedy of Romeo and Juliet*, in which I appeared as the Nurse in a school production at the age of 13. Let's connect at 15MinuteMethod.com/bonus and talk more about that and all the things, shall we?

# Notes

p. 4    *The 100-hour rule, popularized by psychologist Andres Ericsson*: K.A. Ericsson, R.T. Krampe, and C. Tesch-Römer, "The Role of Deliberate Practice in the Acquisition of Expert Performance," *Psychological Review* 100, no. 3 (July 1993): 363–406, https://doi.org/10.1037/0033 -295X.100.3.363.

p. 14   *"Let the beauty we love be what we do"*: Jelaluddin Rumi, *The Essential Rumi*, trans. Coleman Barks (1995; repr., San Francisco: HarperSan-Francisco, 1996), 36.

p. 14   *Studies show that hands-on creativity can lift your mood*: "Creative Activities Help the Brain to Cope with Emotions," University College London News, May 8, 2019, https://www.ucl.ac.uk/news/2019/may /creative-activities-help-brain-cope-emotions.

p. 62   *"inarguably among the top two or three most influential directors and performers"*: Chris Jones, "Review: 'The Comedy of Errors' at Chicago Shakespeare Is a Warm and Generous Farewell from Barbara Gaines," *Chicago Tribune*, March 17, 2023, https://www.chicagotribune.com /entertainment/theater/reviews/ct-ent-comedy-errors-chicago-shakes -review-20230317-b6osvf53l5er7fgr4uri6xx5hi-story.html.

p. 86   *"I wish I'd had the courage to live a life true to myself"*: Bronnie Ware, "Regrets of the Dying," accessed March 1, 2024, https://bronnieware .com/blog/regrets-of-the-dying.

p. 95   *"It's supposed to be hard. If it wasn't hard, everyone would do it."*: Tom Hanks in *A League of Their Own*, audio clip, accessed February 5, 2024, https://movie-sounds.org/famous-movie-samples/quotes-with-sound -clips-from-a-league-of-their-own/it-just-got-too-hard-it-s-supposed -to-be-hard-if-it-wasn-t-hard-everyone-would-do-it-the-hard-is-what -makes-it-great.

p. 101   *"an enlightened witness"*: Alice Miller, "The Essential Role of an Enlightened Witness in Society," 1997, accessed March 1, 2024, https:// www.alice-miller.com/en/the-essential-role-of-an-enlightened-witness -in-society.

p. 101    *"defense is the first act of war"*: Byron Katie often repeats this quote on her socials, for example, Instagram, May 17, 2023: "'Defense is the first act of war.' Why might this be true? xo bk ❤," https://www.instagram .com/p/CsWu7tiMM3T. It also appears in a few of her audio programs and books.

p. 108    *at least 5 percent of their workforce was, that very day, living with depression*: World Health Organization, "Depressive Disorder (Depression)," March 31, 2023, https://www.who.int/news-room/fact-sheets /detail/depression.

p. 111    *"It is true that the materialistic society"*: Thomas Merton, *The Seven Storey Mountain, Fiftieth Anniversary Edition* (Orlando, FL: Harvest, 1999), 147–48.

p. 112    *The counts of the indictment are luxury*: Kenneth John Freeman, *Schools of Hellas: An Essay on the Practice and Theory of Ancient Greek Education from 600 to 300 BC* (London: Macmillan and Co., 1908), 74.

p. 112    *"he was presenting his own summary of the complaints"*: "Misbehaving Children in Ancient Times," Quote Investigator, May 1, 2010, https://quoteinvestigator.com/2010/05/01/misbehave.

p. 121    *77 percent of employees are disengaged*: Megan Cerullo, "More Than Half of Employees Are Disengaged, or 'Quiet Quitting' Their Jobs," CBSNews.com Moneywatch, June 13, 2023, https://www.cbsnews .com/news/workers-disengaged-quiet-quitting-their-jobs-gallup.

p. 143    *"nonviolent communication" as pioneered by Marshall B. Rosenberg, PhD*: See the Center for Nonviolent Communication, https://www.cnvc.org.

p. 144    *There is also such a thing as "agitated depression"*: Kara Mayer Robinson, "What Is Agitated Depression?," WebMD, July 20, 2023, https://www.webmd.com/depression/agitated-depression.

p. 144    *According to the CDC, one in three adults reports not getting enough sleep*: "What Are Sleep Deprivation and Deficiency?," National Heart, Lung, and Blood Institute, last updated March 24, 2022, https://www .nhlbi.nih.gov/health/sleep-deprivation.

p. 145    *It's been reported that 75 percent of Americans are chronically dehydrated*: Chris Furnari, "Are Americans Dehydrated? These Brands Think So," *Forbes*, April 6, 2021, https://www.forbes.com/sites/chrisfurnari /2021/04/06/are-americans-dehydrated-these-brands-think-so /?sh=7c7de30ae080.

p. 153    *approximately 20 percent of small businesses fail within their first year*: USA Link System, "Small Business Statistics 2022 Recap: What Is the Small Business Failure/Success Rate," LinkedIn, March 31, 2023, https://www.linkedin.com/pulse/small-business-statistics-2022-recap -what-failuresuccess.

p. 153 *Only 4 percent of businesses the size of mine make over $250,000 in annual revenue*: Angela Petulla, "2024 Small Business Revenue Statistics," altLINE, last updated January 9, 2024, https://altline.sobanco.com /small-business-revenue-statistics.

p. 155 *average salary of $60,000*: Afifa Mushtaque, "Average Salary in Each State in US," July 26, 2023, https://finance.yahoo.com/news/average -salary-state-us-152311356.html#.

# About the Author

Originally from Chicago, Sam Bennett is a writer, speaker, and creativity/productivity specialist and the author of the best-selling *Get It Done: From Procrastination to Creative Genius in 15 Minutes a Day* and *Start Right Where You Are: How Little Changes Can Make a Big Difference for Overwhelmed Procrastinators, Frustrated Overachievers, and Recovering Perfectionists.*

Having spent most of her life working as a professional actor and improvisor, Sam brings her quick wit to all her work, including the script she wrote for the hit musical *In a Booth at Chasen's.* Recently, she has leveraged her good-humored and down-to-earth teachings to become a top instructor on LinkedIn Learning with over a million learners worldwide. She now lives happily in an old house with three cats, which is just how she always imagined it might be.

Find out more at TheRealSamBennett.com.